AMERICAN RIGHTS

RIGHT TO BEAR ARMS

GERALDINE WOODS

Facts On File, Inc.

Right to Bear Arms

Facts On File, Inc.
132 West 31st Street
New York NY 10001

Library of Congress Cataloging-in-Publication Data
Woods, Geraldine.
　　Right to Bear Arms / Geraldine Woods.
　　　　p. cm. — (American Rights)
　　Includes bibliographical references and index.
　　ISBN 0-8160-5666-8 (alk. paper)
　　1. Firearms—Law and legislation—United States. 2. Gun control—United States. 3. Soldiers—United States—Billeting 4. Constitutional law—United States. I. Title. II. Series.
　　KF3941.W66 2005
　　344.7302'33—dc22　　　　　　　　　　　　2004015721

Facts On File books are available at special discounts when purchased in bulk quantities for businesses, associations, institutions, or sales promotions. Please call our Special Sales Department in New York at (212) 967-8800 or (800) 322-8755.

You can find Facts On File on the World Wide Web at http://www.factsonfile.com

Text design by Erika K. Arroyo
Cover design by Pehrsson Design
Maps and graphs by Sholto Ainslie

Printed in the United States of America

VB FOF 10 9 8 7 6 5 4 3 2 1

This book is printed on acid-free paper.

Note on Photos

Many of the illustrations and photographs used in this book are old, historical images. The quality of the prints is not always up to current standards, as in some cases the originals are from old or poor-quality negatives or are damaged. The content of the illustrations, however, made their inclusion important despite problems in reproduction.

Contents

Introduction   ix

**1 The English Origins of the Right to
Bear Arms and Not to Quarter Troops**   **1**

British Settlement, 18th century   *2*

The Saxon *Fyrd:* An Early Militia   3

English Political Philosophers on the Right
to Bear Arms   8

2 Arms and Troops in Early America   **9**

A Requirement to Bear Arms   11

Prerevolutionary America, 1763   *14*

The States Address Quartering and the Right
to Bear Arms   16

**3 Quartering and the Right to Bear Arms
in the New Nation**   **19**

States vs. Federal Power   19

The States Propose Changes   25

Ratification of the Constitution, 1787–1790   *26*

**4 The Second Amendment and
Gun Control Laws**   **30**

The Roaring Twenties and Gun Control   31

Interstate Commerce and Gun Control   33
The Gun Show Issue   36
The Bradys Behind the Brady Bill   39
State Licensing and Registration Laws, 2004   41
State Laws Regarding the "Right to Carry" a
   Concealed Handgun, 2004   42
Juvenile Handgun Possession Laws, 2004   43
Child Access Protection Laws, by State, 2004   44

5 **The Second and Third Amendments in**
   the Courts   45
How Court Cases Are Named   45
How Court Rulings Are Applied   55
Kennesaw, Georgia   57
Gun Manufacturer Suits   59

6 **Guns in the United States Today**   62
Types of Guns and Ammunition   63
Olympic Accuracy   65
State Constitutions Granting the Right to
   Bear Arms, 2004   66
Where Criminals Get Guns, 1997   67
Crime Victims Injured When Using
   Various Methods of Self-defense, 1997   68
Crimes Committed with Firearms, 1973–2002   70
Murder Weapons, 2002   70
How Murders Are Committed, 1998–2002   71
Murder of Law Enforcement Personnel,
   1973–2000   72
Public Opinion and Gun Control   73

7 **The Case for Gun Control**   75
Assassinations and Attempted Assasssinations
   of U.S. Leaders   78
Murders by People Using Handguns in
   Selected Countries, 1998   80

When Strict Gun Controls Are in Effect:
  The Path to a Permit   81
Pro–Gun Control Activists in Congress   83

8 The Case Against Gun Control   85
   Gun Safety for Young People   90
   Charlton Heston: Actor and Activist   92

9 The Second and Third Amendments Today
   and in the Future   94
   Improving Background Checks   98
   Firearms Fingerprints and Smart Guns   100
   Do Firearms Laws Work?   104

Glossary   107

Chronology   111

Appendix. *Excerpts from Documents Relating
   to the Right to Bear Arms and Not to
   Quarter Troops*   *121*

Further Reading   129

Bibliography   130

Index   137

Introduction

In the National Archives in Washington, D.C., rest some pieces of paper more than 200 years old. Yellowed and faded, these documents—the Constitution of the United States and the Bill of Rights—contain more than the words inked upon them. They carry the hopes for their country's future of a long-dead generation of Americans. They also hold a guarantee of America's most basic freedoms.

The Bill of Rights is made up of 10 amendments, or changes, to the U.S. Constitution. The Second Amendment is a brief statement:

A well regulated Militia, being necessary to the security of a free State, the right of the people to keep and bear Arms shall not be infringed [violated].

It is short but not simple. Since those words were written, millions more have been spoken or printed about the Second Amendment's meaning. The Third Amendment, on the other hand, has attracted very little attention in modern times. When the country was founded, however, the issue of quartering, or placing soldiers in private homes, was very important to Americans. The Third Amendment declares:

No soldier shall, in time of peace be quartered in any house, without the consent of the Owner, nor in time of war but in a manner to be prescribed [approved] by law.

This American right is based on a very old tradition: A homeowner is in control of what goes on inside his or her house. The

The Bill of Rights guarantees basic freedoms to Americans. *(National Archives)*

government, except in times of grave danger, should therefore not place soldiers in private homes unless the residents voluntarily open their doors.

INDIVIDUAL OR GROUP RIGHT?

The argument about the Second Amendment centers on gun control and whether the government has the right to pass laws regulating who may own a gun and how that gun may be bought, sold, or used. Every time a new gun law is passed or a major crime is committed with firearms, the arguments flare up again. The

A poster from World War I recruits members of the National Guard, the United States's modern militia. *(National Archives, U.S. Food Administration)*

disagreement about the Second Amendment centers on one point: whether the Second Amendment gives the right to bear arms to state governments or to individual Americans.

According to one reading of the Second Amendment, the right to keep and bear arms belongs to the citizens of each state as a group. The Second Amendment, interpreted this way, guarantees that each of the U.S. states has the ability to defend itself with an armed force, or militia. Furthermore, the state, but not the individual, has the right to keep and bear arms in its militia. This reading of the Second Amendment is sometimes called the "militia view." In the militia view, the government may decide whether a particular citizen may own a gun and how that gun may be bought, sold, or used. Thus, Americans who favor gun control laws tend to accept the militia view of the Second Amendment.

The opposing position is that the Second Amendment gives the right to keep and bear arms to individual Americans. The founders of the nation, according to this reading, understood that unarmed

A cowboy aims his rifle at a herd of buffalo. *(National Archives, Department of the Interior)*

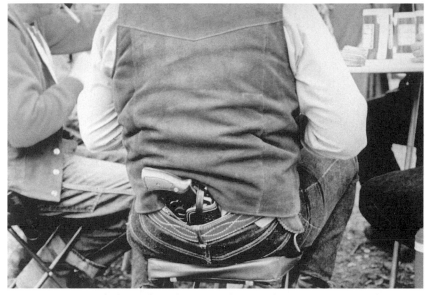

Many Americans believe that the Second Amendment guarantees their right to own a firearm. *(National Archives, Environmental Protection Agency)*

citizens cannot defend themselves or oppose a government that takes away their freedom. This interpretation, often called the "individual rights view" of the Second Amendment, makes most gun control laws unconstitutional.

When the Second and Third Amendments were written, the founders of the nation could not possibly have imagined life in the 21st century. Interpreting these rights is the task of lawmakers, the courts, and citizens of the American democracy.

1

The English Origins of the Right to Bear Arms and Not to Quarter Troops

Most of the colonists in the territory that would eventually become the United States of America traced their roots to the British Isles. Therefore, it is not surprising that established legal principles, also known as common law, were specifically recognized in the charters of almost all the British colonies in North America. Thus, the origin of the right to bear arms and not to quarter troops lies across the Atlantic, in England.

STANDING ARMIES AND MILITIAS

To English citizens of the Middle Ages (ca. A.D. 500–1500), the right to keep and bear arms and the right not to quarter troops were part of a larger issue: the roles of a "standing" army and a militia. For most of its history, each community in England defended itself with a loosely organized local fighting force, or militia. In the 11th century, Normans from France conquered the Saxons. They divided the country into large estates, each with a noble in charge. The nobles were commanded to keep a certain number of knights armed and ready for royal service. They also had to pay a tax so that the sovereign, the king or queen, could equip and train royal soldiers. The sovereign's soldiers were under direct control of the throne, but the knights owed their first loyalty to the nobles. Power struggles between the nobles and the sovereign were frequent. The knights represented local control. The royal "standing" army was the force behind the sovereign's centralized power.

> "Let an Englishman go where he will, he carries as much of [English] law and liberty with him as the nature of things will bear."
>
> —*Richard West, an official in the American colonies, in 1720*

1

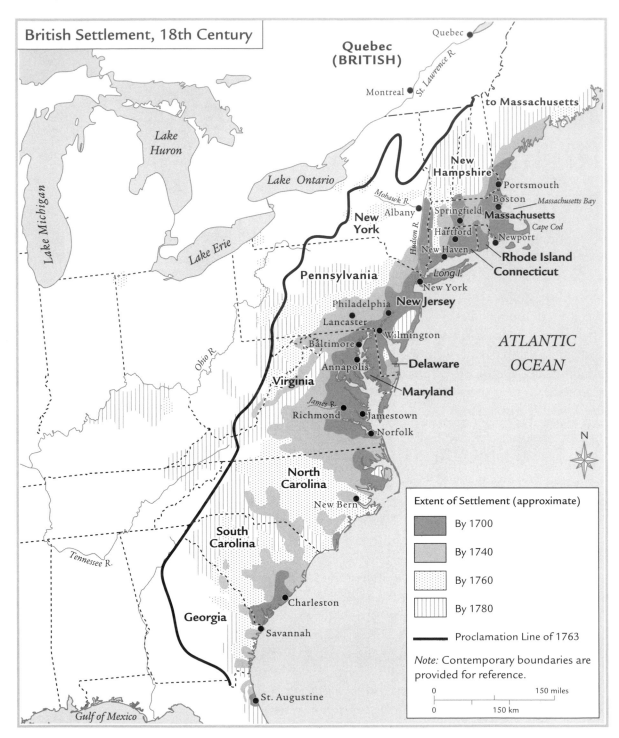

British Settlement, 18th Century

Quebec
(BRITISH)

Quebec

Lake
Huron

Lake Ontario

Montreal

St. Lawrence R.

to Massachusetts

New
Hampshire

Portsmouth
Boston

Massachusetts Bay

Lake Michigan

Lake Erie

Mohawk R.

Albany

Springfield

Massachusetts

Hudson R.

New
York

Hartford

Cape Cod

Newport

New Haven

Rhode Island

Pennsylvania

Long I.

Connecticut

New York

New Jersey

Philadelphia

Ohio R.

Lancaster

Wilmington

Baltimore

Delaware

Annapolis

Virginia

Maryland

James R.

Richmond

Jamestown

Norfolk

ATLANTIC
OCEAN

N

North
Carolina

New Bern

South
Carolina

Tennessee R.

Extent of Settlement (approximate)

By 1700

By 1740

By 1760

By 1780

Charleston

Georgia

Savannah

Proclamation Line of 1763

Note: Contemporary boundaries are
provided for reference.

0   150 miles

St. Augustine

0   150 km

Gulf of Mexico

Most of the territory that eventually became the United States was settled by the British.

THE SAXON *FYRD*
An Early Militia

Until the 11th century the territory now known as England was inhabited and ruled by Saxons. When soldiers were needed for defense, the Saxons relied on the local *fyrd*. The *fyrd* was a militia, a group of amateur soldiers called together in time of emergency. All able-bodied Saxon men were members of the *fyrd;* they were required to bring their own weapons if their region was attacked. Service in the *fyrd* was for short periods of time; when the danger was over, the militiamen went back to their homes and usual occupations. A few important nobles kept professional soldiers on the payroll, but no national army stood waiting for the day it was needed.

Under Norman rule, most adult male citizens were part of civilian militias that could be called upon by the noble in charge of that area of the country. The king or queen had the right to summon these citizen soldiers when needed. Local militias also served as a check on the power of the royal army. If the ruler overstepped and oppressed the subjects, an armed militia might, and sometimes did, rebel. Therefore, when English sovereigns wanted to increase royal power and influence, a first step was to disarm or control the militia.

The struggle for power between militias and standing armies was especially intense during the 17th century, a time of great unrest in England. Several governments were overthrown by force during this period. Relations were strained between Parliament, the English lawmaking body, and the sovereign. In 1642, for example, Parliament was determined not to give too much control to the sovereign. It passed a law giving itself control over the militias. Charles II came to power in 1660 after two governments had been overthrown. He gathered as much power for himself as he possibly could. Early in his reign, Charles II signed the Militia Act, placing the Crown in control of the militias and disbanding those thought likely to revolt. He also enacted a number of laws designed to take weapons away from ordinary citizens.

King Charles II (reigned 1660–85) placed England's militias under royal control. He also limited ordinary citizens' access to firearms. *(Library of Congress, Prints and Photographs Division [LC-USZ62-96910])*

Charles's successor, James II, passed still more laws to disarm his subjects. He also created a large, powerful standing army. Thanks to Charles II's Militia Act, the king already controlled the local militias. Thus people who opposed the king's policies had little means of resistance. To many citizens, James's standing army became a symbol of tyranny, or unchecked royal power.

In the 18th century, English, Scottish, and Welsh citizens, united in 1707 under the throne of Great Britain, gradually came to accept the need for a professional army. Weapons and battle tactics had become more sophisticated than they were in earlier centuries. It was clear that if Britain was attacked, temporary militia fighters would be no match for the trained career soldiers of other countries. Nevertheless, respect for the militia tradition remained strong, especially in Britain's American colonies.

THE RIGHT NOT TO QUARTER TROOPS

Modern-day soldiers tend to live on bases or in government housing; throughout much of history, though, soldiers had no specialized camps. In England, when troops passed through an area, army officers forced homeowners to provide them food and shelter. This practice is known as quartering. Citizens were supposed to be paid for the goods used by soldiers, but all too often the homeowner received no money at all. In fact, troops were often accused of stealing and other abuses. Forced quartering gave townspeople another reason to favor their own local knights and militia and to hate standing armies.

As the royal standing armies grew in size and importance, the number of complaints about their behavior also increased. Homeowners began to demand protection from forced quartering. Beginning in the 12th century, many English cities and towns negotiated royal charters that limited the powers of the king and spelled out some rights that could not be taken from citizens. These charters contained the distant ancestors of the Third Amendment. The first official ban on forced quartering was a charter for the city of London granted in 1130 during the reign of Henry I. The charter said that no royal soldier would be quartered "within the walls of the city . . . by force."

The London charter, like most other English charters, banned only forced quartering. If a homeowner agreed, soldiers could still be housed in private residences. This latter practice is known as voluntary quartering. The army issued payment documents to be exchanged for money or tax relief. In practice, the payment requests were often denied, and quartering—voluntary or forced—remained an issue for centuries. In 1628, for example, Parliament listed the injustices they wanted the king to remedy, including the fact that English citizens "against their wills" had been forced to

"Your majesty would be pleased to remove said soldiers . . . that your people may not be so burdened in time to come."

—*statement by Parliament to the king in 1628*

The British redcoats (soldiers) clashed with American rebels in 1770. Redcoats were sometimes quartered in the homes of colonists. *(National Archives, Works Projects Administration)*

quarter "great companies of soldiers and mariners [sailors]." The lawmakers asked for an end to quartering.

In 1679, Parliament passed the Anti-Quartering Act, which prohibited troops from being quartered in private homes in both peace and wartime. Yet one of the complaints about King James II was that he had violated the anti-quartering law. For that reason and many others, James lost his throne in 1688. In 1689, the new rulers of England, William and Mary, were forced to accept the Declaration of Rights, a direct ancestor of the American Bill of Rights that would be written about a century later. By signing the declaration, William and Mary agreed not to create a standing army without the approval of Parliament. Quartering was not directly prohibited by the declaration, but Parliament soon passed still another law forbidding forced quartering in England. British anti-quartering laws did not apply to the American colonies, however, and in the years leading up to the American Revolution, forced quartering of British soldiers in American homes became one of the colonists' strongest complaints.

THE RIGHT TO KEEP AND BEAR ARMS

Another right guaranteed in the declaration that William and Mary signed was "That the Subjects, which are Protestants may have Arms for their Defence suitable to their Conditions, and as allowed by Law." The right to keep and bear arms did not begin with William and Mary, however. Ordinary English citizens, with some important exceptions, had had access to arms for centuries.

To fulfill their militia duties, male English citizens kept a variety of arms. On reporting for militia or guard duty, each citizen brought his own weapons. The government might provide extra ammunition or arms, but in general the responsibility rested with each individual. Arms were also necessary for the protection of homes and families. The first professional police force in Britain was not formed until the 19th century. Before that time, adult men between the ages of 16 and 60 were supposed to take to the streets for guard duty or to catch wrongdoers whenever the alarm was raised.

Some English rulers actually ordered their subjects to keep and bear arms. During the reign of King Alfred the Great in the ninth century, for example, the law specified that able-bodied citizens arm themselves at their own expense. In 1181, Henry II ordered every freeman to own a weapon, in case the king needed to call out the militia. He commanded his wealthy subjects to "have a coat of mail, a helmet, a shield, and a lance." Those who owned less property were to acquire only a sleeveless metal vest, a cap of iron, and a lance. In 1511, King Henry VIII commanded his subjects to possess and train with longbows. Henry's daughter Queen Mary I required civilian militias to carry their own firearms.

LIMITATIONS ON THE RIGHT TO BEAR ARMS

The tradition of keeping and bearing arms, however, was not unlimited. English citizens had always been subject to restrictions on the possession and use of weapons. In 1328, the Statute (law) of Northampton stated that "no man great nor small [shall] . . . go nor ride armed by Night nor by Day, in Fairs, Market, nor in the Presence of the Justices or other ministers." It also specified that Englishmen could not "go armed to the terror of the populace." In other words, unless on military or police duty Englishmen were not to carry their weapons in public places or to use arms to frighten others.

In 1383, Richard II ordered his subjects not to carry arms while riding. About 100 years later, Henry VII outlawed the wheelock, the first gun to ignite gunpowder with a spark. In the 16th century, Henry VIII banned crossbows and handguns, which were often used by highway robbers, for everyone who earned less than 100 pounds a year. As that was a large sum of money, only the richest Englishmen could possess these weapons legally. However, almost everyone was allowed a gun that was more than a yard long, as large firearms could not easily be hidden for criminal purposes. Catholics, whom Henry VIII considered his enemies, were prohibited almost all weapons. (Catholics were also denied arms during the reigns of many other English sovereigns.) Also in the 16th century, King Edward VI commanded "all persons who shoot guns" to register with local authorities; other rulers of this period strictly regulated gun shops and banned the importation of guns or gun parts from other countries.

> "Every man between 15 years of age and 60 years of age shall be assessed [have his wealth counted] and sworn to armor according to the quantity of their lands and goods; that is . . . from 15 pounds Lands and Goods . . . a sword, a knife, and a horse."
>
> —*Statute of Winchester, issued by King Edward I in 1285*

ENGLISH POLITICAL PHILOSOPHERS ON THE RIGHT TO BEAR ARMS

Sir William Blackstone, an English political philosopher and historian, wrote in 1765 that one "of the absolute rights of individuals . . . is that of having arms for their defence." Blackstone, drawing on England's experience with the militia and the standing army, argued that only an armed citizenry could really be free. Civilian militias, wrote Blackstone, curbed the ruler's power and protected the people from tyranny. In 1780, the recorder (an English official) stated that "the right of his majesty's Protestant subjects to have arms for their own defence, and to use them for lawful purposes, is most clear and undeniable." However, the recorder also noted that there were limits on the legal use of arms and these limits changed according to the circumstances. Andrew Fletcher, another English political writer of the 18th century, stated that a good militia is "the chief part of the constitution of any free government."

British settlers brought a deep distrust for standing armies and a respect for a civilian militia to the New World. A long tradition of keeping and bearing arms and an equally long tradition of arms regulation also came with the colonists. The North American colonies, however, were quite different from the measured fields and settled towns of the Old World. Like almost every other aspect of life, the right to bear arms and not to quarter soldiers had to adapt to conditions in America.

2

Arms and Troops in Early America

Throughout the age of exploration and colonization, in the 1600s and 1700s, for the most part in England only men of property owned and used firearms. But in the American colonies the situation was different. A British visitor to the New World wrote that one could not find "a Man born in America that does not understand the Use of Firearms." He added that a gun was "almost the First thing they Purchase and take to all the New Settlements and in the cities you can scarcely find a Lad of twelve years That does not go a Gunning."

A USEFUL WEAPON

Not every historian agrees, but most scholars think that gun ownership in the colonies was widespread, a basic part of the early American experience. Firearms were needed for many reasons. North America was largely wilderness when the European colonists arrived. The forests teemed with wildlife, such as bears, deer, mountain lions, and other animals. Some observers noted that at times the sky was actually darkened by huge flocks of birds flying overhead. Firearms were useful in hunting game for food. Furthermore, the settlers were open to attack whenever they left the cleared spaces of farms and towns. Guns helped the colonists survive when dangerous animals menaced them.

Guns also gave the colonists an advantage over the earliest inhabitants of North America, the American Indians. The areas settled by immigrants from Europe had already been populated for many years by American Indians, but the European settlers did not recognize the property rights of the original inhabitants. At first,

Geronimo, an Apache, holds a rifle in 1887. In the colonial era, Native Americans were not allowed to own guns, although this law was frequently broken. (*National Archives, Department of Defense*)

many Indian tribes cooperated with the newcomers, but as more and more settlers arrived and seized land, American Indians increasingly turned to violence to protect their homes, families, and way of life.

No American Indians possessed firearms when the first Europeans arrived. Many tribes acquired guns eventually, despite laws in almost every colony prohibiting Europeans from selling or trading firearms to American Indians. Nor were American Indians the only armed threat to British colonists. The wars of the Old World between the British and the French, Dutch, or Spanish frequently spread to the North American continent. More trouble arose in the New World as the Europeans competed for land. For most of the colonial period, firearms were the settlers' best defense against attacks from both American Indians and hostile Europeans.

ARMED BY LAW

Firearms in the colonial period were imported from Europe and were extremely expensive. A good musket cost almost as much as the average monthly income of

In the colonial era, ordinary citizens, such as these churchgoers pictured here, often carried guns to protect themselves from attacks. (*Collection of the New-York Historical Society*)

A REQUIREMENT TO BEAR ARMS

At times in early America, some colonists were required to own firearms. In 1623, the Plymouth colony passed a law stating that "every freeman or other inhabitant of this colony [must] provide for himselfe and each under him able to beare armes a sufficient musket and other serviceable piece of war." The Massachusetts Bay Colony lent money to any militiaman who could not afford a gun; the price of the gun had to be repaid as soon as the militiaman was able. In the colony of New York, every man was supposed to "provide himself, at his own Expense, with a good musket or Firelock, a sufficient Bayonet and Belt, a pouch with . . . not less than Twenty-Four Cartridges . . . two spare Flints, a Blanket and Knapsack." An 18th-century Connecticut regulation stated that all male citizens "always be provided with and have in continual readiness, a well-fixed firelock . . . or other good firearms . . . a good sword, or cutlass . . . one pound of good powder, four pounds of bullets fit for his gun, and twelve flints."

a middle-class settler. Nevertheless, American lawmakers so feared attacks from American Indians or other enemies that colonial governments quickly organized militias modeled on the militias in Britain. The militias, for the most part, were not provided with weapons. Instead, the militiamen were expected to supply their own firearms.

But it was not enough simply to own firearms. Many colonies ordered men to carry their weapons when attacks were likely. Virginia commanded that "no man go or send abroad without a sufficient partie well armed." A 1770 Georgia law forced men to take their guns to church, in case of an American Indian raid. Religious officials were empowered to search each man up to 14 times a year to be sure that he carried the necessary weapon.

On the other hand, many local governments prohibited citizens from bearing weapons during times of peace. Firearms might be stored in a locked building, to be removed only in crisis or for muster, a militia drill. After some colonial militias revolted against their local governments, a number of colonies prohibited private citizens from carrying guns or other arms in public. The legal code

"The People there [in Virginia] are very Skillful in the use of Fire-Arms, being all their Lives accustom'd to shoot in the Wood."

—*Virginian Robert Beverley, 1705, writing about the Virginia colony*

of most colonies barred hunting or shooting on town streets and using a gun to frighten or threaten citizens.

A LIMITED RIGHT

Laws requiring citizens to keep and bear arms did not apply to everyone. Males under the age of 16 and over 60 were not covered by these laws, nor were females of any age. Women's roles during this period were quite different from those of men. Colonial laws simply ignored women on this issue because it was understood that women did not handle guns.

Nonwhites were generally not allowed to own firearms. Slavery was legal and common in colonial America. Blacks were frequently barred from possessing weapons for fear of slave revolts. Even free blacks were prohibited firearms in some states, perhaps because lawmakers worried that free blacks would join with the slaves to overthrow white slave masters. A Virginia statute called for men who were "capable of arms (excepting Negroes)" to obtain "arms both offensive and defensive." To keep weapons out of the hands of slaves, the colony of South Carolina required white owners to lock up firearms. Most militias would not accept nonwhite members, although in times of crisis, these rules might be ignored.

American Indians were also subject to gun prohibitions. According to the laws of Jamestown, Virginia, settlers who sold or gave firearms to American Indians could be hanged. In 1641, the central government in England ruled that no guns were to be sold or traded to American Indians. Like all rules, this one was sometimes broken. American Indians quickly understood the advantage of muskets, rifles, and gunpowder. Similarly, some colonists, more concerned about profit than the law, grasped how much money could be made by selling weapons. Also, at times a colonial government armed friendly Indian tribes so that they could battle tribes that were enemies of the colony.

In some areas, members of a minority religious or ethnic group were barred from gun ownership. In the mid-18th century, for example, Maryland did not permit Catholics to possess guns. In the same way, New England officials denied arms to Catholics and to dissenters, that is, anyone who did not accept the local established faith. When British forces took New York from the Dutch in 1674,

"In trading with the Indians, no man shall give them . . . any weapons of war, either guns or gunpowder, or sword, nor any other Munition [weapon], which might come to be used against ourselves."

—*1641 decree by the English Crown restricting gun sales or trade with Native Americans*

Major Edmund Andros, the new governor, gathered all firearms and forbade Dutch residents access to these weapons.

As relations between Great Britain and the American colonies became strained, some colonies passed laws forbidding firearms to Tories, or settlers loyal to the British Crown. One town assembly passed a resolution that anyone who would not "defend American rights" be disarmed. Other colonies allowed firearms only to those who, in the words of Boston resident Josiah Quincy, showed "an interest in the safety of the community."

THE MILITIA AS A DEFENSE AGAINST TYRANNY

The issue of firearms was closely related to the roles of the colonial militia and the standing army of professional British soldiers. True to their British roots, many colonists condemned standing armies

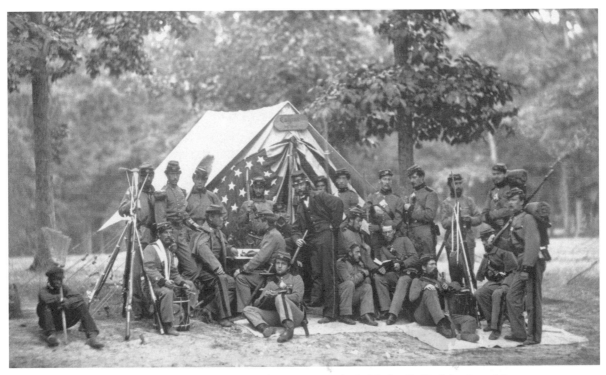

Each American colony protected itself with a militia composed of able-bodied adult men. After independence, many states continued to support militias. This 1865 photo shows men from the New York State militia. *(National Archives, War Department)*

Prerevolutionary America, 1763

The thirteen colonies became the original states of the Union after the Revolutionary War.

and praised the militia, just as ordinary English citizens had done back in the Old World. Samuel Stillman, a colonial minister, wrote in 1770 that the militia was "the security of a country." A pamphlet published by an American Patriot in 1758 put the issue another way, arguing that "every Freeman and every Freeholder should be a Soldier" in order to defend the rights of citizens against tyranny.

Royal officials, meanwhile, saw the colonial militia as a possible threat to the British Crown. When the American settlers moved toward more independence from Britain, British colonial undersecretary William Knox wrote a pamphlet entitled "What Is Fit to Be Done with America?" He argued that the militia laws "should be repealed and . . . the Arms of all the People should be taken away."

The British government did not immediately follow Knox's advice, but throughout the 18th century it did send more and more troops to the American colonies to fight the Seven Years' War against the French. The colonists may have welcomed British soldiers—known as redcoats, for their uniform—during wartime, but Americans deeply resented the army's presence once peace was restored. In 1774, Thomas Jefferson expressed the views of most Americans when he condemned King George III for keeping "among us large bodies of armed forces, not made up of the people here, nor raised by the authority of our laws."

Jefferson's words reflected a deep difference between the way Britain viewed America and the way the colonists saw themselves. To the British, the colonies existed for the benefit of the mother country. To the Americans, the colonies were home, where they expected to enjoy the rights and privileges of all British citizens, including the right to keep and bear arms and not to quarter soldiers. The standing British army represented a threat to the American colonies' self-rule and traditional liberties.

THE COLONISTS RESENT QUARTERING

In the winter and spring of 1774–75, the movement urging independence from Britain gained strength. Throughout the thirteen colonies, Americans at assemblies and conventions passed resolutions condemning a number of actions taken by the British government, including the stationing of a standing army of British

"Whenever governments mean to invade the rights and liberties of the people, they always attempt to destroy the militia, in order to raise an army upon their ruins."

—Elbridge Gerry, American Patriot, signer of the Declaration of Independence, 1789

Thomas Jefferson (1743–1826) was the author of the Declaration of Independence. *(National Archives)*

soldiers in America. Much of the trouble stemmed from the quartering of troops.

Quartering had seldom been a problem with the militia. Militiamen were local residents, called up only for a short while whenever danger threatened. Thus militiamen generally slept at home or in makeshift camps. But professional soldiers were not the colonists' friends and neighbors; they were "imports" from Britain. The redcoats served in the colonies for long periods of time, at the expense of local governments and to the inconvenience of citizens. In the 18th century, American officials in many areas refused to vote funds to build barracks or to pay for soldiers' quarters. In response, the British government passed the Quartering Act of 1765, which required the colonists to provide the cost of food and shelter for British soldiers. If no barracks were available, the redcoats were to be quartered in inns, stables, and alehouses. Their expenses were to be paid by the colonies.

THE STATES ADDRESS QUARTERING AND THE RIGHT TO BEAR ARMS

After the Declaration of Independence was signed in 1776, the former colonies called themselves "states" and wrote their own constitutions. Most contained statements protesting standing armies and outlawing forced quartering of soldiers. The Pennsylvania constitution held that "as standing armies in the time of peace are dangerous to liberty, they ought not to be kept up." Delaware stated that "no soldiers ought to be quartered in any house in time of peace without the consent of the owner, and in time of war in such manner only as the legislature shall direct." Maryland, Massachusetts, and New Hampshire allowed standing armies with "the consent of the Legislature." Virginia specifically mentioned the militia, stating that "a well-regulated militia, composed of the body of the people, trained to arms, is the proper, natural, and safe defense of a free State."

In 1776, the thirteen colonies declared their independence from Britain and formed a new nation. The Declaration of Independence is now housed in the National Archives in Washington, D.C. *(National Archives)*

The American colonies bitterly opposed the Quartering Act of 1765. To make matters worse, in 1774, Britain enacted another quartering act, this time specifying that troops could be placed even in private homes. The colonists' anger grew. One newspaper described the "outrageous behavior" of the army, reporting that two women had been struck and one robbed by British soldiers. According to the paper, "such violence [was] always to be . . . [expected] from military troops, when quartered in the body of a populous city."

The troops' behavior was, of course, only part of the problem. The colonists viewed the British soldiers as an occupying army, especially when the soldiers were ordered to seize American guns. In fact, the first battle of the American Revolution was fought in 1775 when the standing Royal Army attempted to take possession of a stockpile of militia firearms in Concord, Massachusetts.

In 1776, the colonies took an important step by issuing the Declaration of Independence. The declaration charged the king with keeping a standing army in America and "quartering large bodies of troops among us." But the Declaration of Independence was only a piece of paper in 1776. The nation could not become a reality until a bloody war had been fought. But long before the last shot of the Revolutionary War had been fired in 1781, the groundwork for two basic American rights—the right to keep and bear arms and not to quarter troops—was in place.

3

Quartering and the Right to Bear Arms in the New Nation

The U.S. Constitution was written more than two centuries ago, in 1787. Except for the Civil War years (1861–65), when it faced serious challenges, the Constitution has been a blueprint for a stable system of government. Yet, when the founders of the nation were crafting the Constitution, they had no way of knowing whether their efforts would meet with success. Fierce fights erupted over almost every aspect of the document.

STATES VS. FEDERAL POWER

The basic question the founders faced was simple: How should power be shared between the states and the new central, "united" government? The former colonists were used to thinking of themselves as New Yorkers, Virginians, Pennsylvanians, and so on, not as citizens of the United States. They had just fought the Revolutionary War against one distant government—the British king and Parliament—that did not respect their right to rule themselves. Now they did not want to give up too much power to another distant body—the central, or federal, government of the United States of America. On the other hand, the Revolutionary War had taught Americans another lesson, as well: Without a strong union such as the one they had created to fight the redcoats, each individual state was weak.

The former colonists wanted something completely new; the royal model from Europe did not interest most Americans. Understandably, Americans wanted to guard their personal freedoms. One cause of the Revolutionary War was the tendency of the Crown to limit the rights that English citizens had traditionally enjoyed. Now that the colonies were free, these rights could be guaranteed. But inventing a new political system was a difficult task. In fact, the founders had to do it twice before they got it right.

THE ARTICLES OF CONFEDERATION

The first government of the United States was organized according to the principles laid down in the Articles of Confederation. The Articles of Confederation arose from a 1774 meeting of the Continental Congress in Philadelphia, Pennsylvania. At the Continental Congress, delegates from each state discussed how to respond to British laws and policies that the colonists opposed. Once the Revolution got under way, the Continental Congress became the only central governing body for the Americans.

In 1775, a subcommittee of the Continental Congress, headed by John Dickinson of Delaware, began to design a national government. In early July 1776, Dickinson's committee presented its work to Congress. The document was entitled the Articles of Confederation. Over the next several years, the governments of each state discussed and voted on the Articles of Confederation. When Maryland accepted the document in 1781, the articles officially went into effect, and the United States had a true federal government for the first time.

The government that Dickinson's committee established strongly supported states' rights. The Articles of Confederation declared that "each State retains [keeps] its sovereignty [right to rule itself], freedom, and independence." The Articles of Confederation also said that the states were members of "a firm league of friendship" that would "assist each other" in case of attack. No national army was provided for. However, the Articles of Confederation held that every state "shall always keep up a well regulated and disciplined militia, sufficiently armed and accoutered [equipped]." The state governments were also supposed to "provide and constantly have ready for use, in public stores, a due number of field pieces and tents, and a proper quantity of arms, ammunition, and camp equipage [equipment]." The militias would allow each state to defend itself in case of attack by another state. If necessary, the state militia could also oppose the central government if federal officials attempted to take away the citizens' rights.

No statement about the right to keep and bear arms or the right to be free from forced quartering was included in the Articles of Confederation. The articles did give the states "every Power . . . and right" not specifically mentioned as belonging to the national government. Possibly the delegates thought that individual state constitutions should take care of the right to bear arms. In fact, some state constitutions had addressed this topic, often with respect to the role of an armed militia. The Virginia constitution had declared that "a well-regulated Militia, composed of the body of the people, trained to arms, is the proper, natural, and safe defense of a free state." The constitution of Pennsylvania stated that "the people have a right to bear arms for the defense of themselves and the state." New York's constitution contained this statement: "The duty of every man who enjoys the protection of society [is] to be prepared and willing to defend it." New York also called for a militia that would be "at all times . . . armed and disciplined."

Some state constitutions, including those of Delaware, Maryland, and Massachusetts, also protected the people from the hated practice of forced quartering. Delaware's statement was typical: "That no soldier ought to be quartered in any house in time of peace without the consent of the owner; and in time of war in such manner only as the Legislature shall direct."

THE CONSTITUTIONAL CONVENTION

The government that the Articles of Confederation created was weak and ineffective. Congress could not tax, for example, but could only ask the states for money. Within a few years, it was obvious that the nation could not survive without a stronger central government. So in 1787, delegates from each state met in Philadelphia once again, this time to write a constitution. As they had in the past, the representatives split into two camps, those favoring a limited central government with maximum power given to the states and those favoring the opposite. The strong central government supporters were called Federalists. Their opponents were called anti-Federalists or states' righters.

The Constitution of the United States was created in Independence Hall in Philadelphia, Pennsylvania. *(Library of Congress, Prints and Photographs Division [LC-USZ61-1147])*

All through the summer of 1787—one of the hottest in memory—the delegates argued over their country's future. Benjamin Franklin, the oldest member of the convention, reminded the delegates that a carpenter often has to shave a bit from both sides of a board in order to fit the wood into its proper place. In the same way, the delegates on each side of an issue should be willing to scale back some of their personal demands for the benefit of the whole.

The Constitution, completed in September 1787, established the form of government that the United States currently employs. Both the states' righters and the Federalists achieved some victories, and both groups also suffered some defeats. The issue of a standing army and local militias is a good example of the compromises the founders made. According to Article I, Section 8, of the Constitution, the federal government may "raise and support Armies." However, the armed forces may be financed for only two years at a time. Every other year, Congress must vote to authorize additional money. The idea behind this design was that Congress, representing citizens from every state, could limit the power of the army by controlling its funding.

According to the same section of Article I, each state maintains a militia, but the federal government can call on the militia to uphold the nation's laws, to put down rebellions, and to fight foreign invaders. The federal government must provide for "organizing, arming, and disciplining, the Militia, and for governing such Part of them as may be employed in the Service of the United States." The states, however, are responsible for appointing militia officers. The states train the militias, while Congress sets national standards for this training.

"... the power in the federal legislature, to raise and support armies at pleasure, as well in peace as in war, and their controul [sic] over the militia, tend, not only to a consolidation of the government, but the destruction of liberty."

—*from an anti-Federalist article by "Brutus" published in the* New York Journal, *October 18, 1787*

DEBATES IN THE PRESS

Before the Constitution could become official, it had to be accepted by at least nine of the 13 states. Around the nation, Americans used local newspapers to argue strongly about the merits and disadvantages of the new system. The militia attracted much debate. Patrick Henry of Virginia, a states' righter, worried that the federal government would have too much power over the state militias. "My great objection to this government," he said, "is that it does not leave us the means of defending our rights." George Mason, another states' righter, argued that "there should be an express [clear] declaration that the state governments might arm and discipline the militia." In an anti-Federalist article in the *Independent Gazeteer* of Philadelphia, Samuel Bryan wrote that a standing army would be a "grand engine of oppression," taking rights away from the people and collecting unreasonable taxes by force.

Other Americans, however, spoke and wrote in favor of the Constitution. Three of the most important Federalists—Alexander Hamilton, John Jay, and James Madison—wrote a series of newspaper

"The governments [of Europe] are afraid to trust the people with arms. . . . But were the people to possess the additional advantages of local governments chosen by themselves, who could collect the national will, and direct the national force; and of officers appointed out of the militia . . . the throne of every tyranny in Europe would be speedily overturned, in spite of the legions [soldiers] which surround it."

—*from* The Federalist Papers, *essay no. 46 (written by James Madison), January 29, 1788*

Patrick Henry (1736–99) was a fierce supporter of states' rights. *(National Archives)*

Alexander Hamilton (1757–1804) favored a strong central government. *(National Archives)*

"... people oppressed and dispirited, neither possess arms nor know how to use them. Tyrants never feel secure, until they have disarmed the people. They can rely upon nothing but stand-ing armies of . . . troops for the support of their power. But the people of this country have arms in their hands; they are not . . . [lacking] military knowledge; every citizen is required by Law to be a soldier . . . for the defence of our country."

—from an anti-Federalist article in the Connecticut Courant, *January 7, 1788*

articles that were published throughout the country. Their writings, published under the name Publius, became known as *The Federalist Papers.* One article stated that local militias would more than balance the power of a national army. The writer presented an image of "a militia amounting to near half a million citizens with arms in their hands, officered by men chosen from among themselves, fighting for their common liberties." The writer went on to say, "It may well be doubted whether [such] a militia . . . could ever be conquered by . . . regular troops."

Noah Webster, another famous Patriot, also defended the Constitution. Webster wrote, "Before a standing army can rule, the people must be disarmed, as they are in almost every kingdom in Europe. The supreme power in America cannot enforce unjust laws by the sword; because the whole body of the people are armed, and constitute a force superior to any band of regular troops that can be, on any pretence, raised in the United States."

DEBATES IN STATE CONVENTIONS

In every one of the 13 states, delegates assembled to discuss and vote on the proposed Constitution. Those who favored ratification, or acceptance, had the advantage. The system they favored was already laid out for the inspection of the voters, right there in the document that had been written in Philadelphia. Those who opposed the plan had nothing ready to replace the Constitution. They could only argue against the Philadelphia proposal, listening in turn to the favorable arguments of the Federalists.

And argue they did. Much of the discussion centered on the Constitution's lack of a bill of rights. Many state constitutions already contained such a section listing specific protections for the traditional freedoms of citizens established under English law. Nine state constitutions specifically mentioned the right to bear arms or provided for an armed militia, and some also addressed quartering. Opponents of the Constitution feared that without a bill of rights, the new body of law would not protect Americans from tyranny. One delegate commented that with the Constitution as originally written, Congress "at their pleasure may arm or disarm all or any part of the freemen of the United States."

THE STATES PROPOSE CHANGES

Many delegates at the state conventions wrote amendments, or changes for the federal Constitution. New Hampshire, for example, called for an amendment "that no standing army shall be kept up in time of peace, unless with the consent of three-quarters of the members of each branch of Congress—nor shall soldiers in time of peace be quartered upon private houses, without the consent of the owners." New Hampshire further proposed that "Congress shall never disarm any citizen, unless such as are or have been in actual rebellion." Pennsylvania wrote that "the people have a right to bear arms for the defence of themselves and their own state, or the United States, or for the purpose of killing game; and no law shall be passed for disarming the people or any of them, unless for crimes committed, or real danger of public injury from individuals." New York declared that "the people have a right to keep and bear arms; that a well regulated militia, including the body of the people capable of bearing arms, is the proper, natural, and safe defence of a free state." New York also condemned standing armies and stated that "no soldier ought to be quartered in any house without the consent of the owner; and in time of war only by the civil magistrate, in such manner as the laws may direct." North Carolina and Virginia passed resolutions similar to New York's.

THE BILL OF RIGHTS

Several points became clear as delegates in state after state debated the Constitution. Most states were willing to accept the new system of government, but only if a bill of rights was added to the document. In fact, New York, Massachusetts, and Virginia would not accept the Constitution until the Federalists promised to amend it at the first opportunity. North Carolina and Rhode Island refused ratification until the amendments were actually approved. Accordingly, the founders gathered once again to create 10 amendments, the Bill of Rights. These statements form the framework for America's liberty.

There was little debate about the Second Amendment. James Madison, one of the writers of the Constitution, drafted this

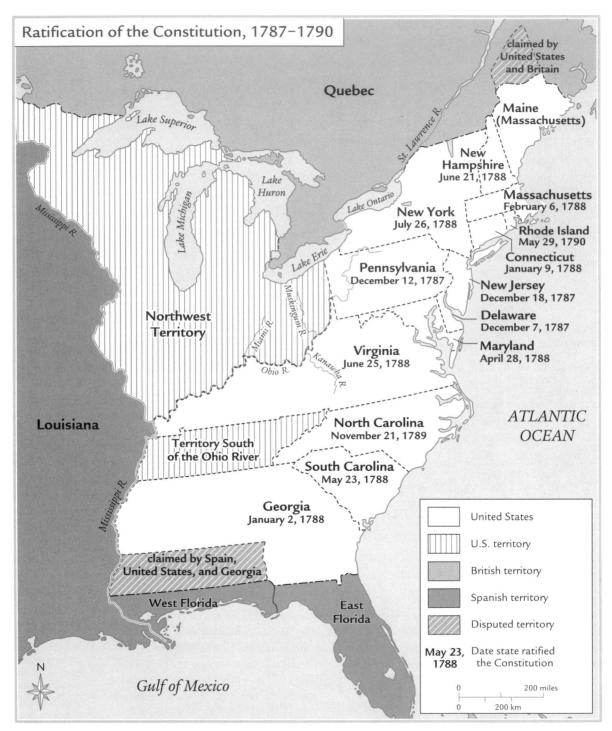

Ratification of the Constitution, 1787–1790

claimed by
United States
and Britain

Quebec

Maine
(Massachusetts)

Lake Superior

New
Hampshire
June 21, 1788

Lake Michigan   *Lake Huron*

Massachusetts
February 6, 1788

Lake Ontario

Lake Erie

New York
July 26, 1788

Rhode Island
May 29, 1790

Connecticut
January 9, 1788

Pennsylvania
December 12, 1787

New Jersey
December 18, 1787

Mississippi R.

Northwest
Territory

Muskingum R.

Miami R.

Delaware
December 7, 1787

Maryland
April 28, 1788

Ohio R.   *Kanawha R.*

Virginia
June 25, 1788

Louisiana

ATLANTIC
OCEAN

Territory South
of the Ohio River

North Carolina
November 21, 1789

South Carolina
May 23, 1788

Mississippi R.

Georgia
January 2, 1788

claimed by Spain,
United States, and Georgia

West Florida

East
Florida

N

Gulf of Mexico

	United States
	U.S. territory
	British territory
	Spanish territory
	Disputed territory
May 23, 1788	Date state ratified the Constitution

0   200 miles
0   200 km

The Constitution was ratified, or accepted, by the 13 original states between 1787 and 1790.

Many delegates to the Constitutional Convention were wary of creating a standing army. In the years following, however, Americans have come to accept the need for a strong and prepared armed forces. This World War II recruiting poster emphasizes the need to defend U.S. interests. *(National Archives, Department of the Navy)*

version: "The right of the people to keep and bear arms shall not be infringed; a well armed and well regulated militia being the best security of a free country; but no person religiously scrupulous of

Elbridge Gerry (1744–1814) was a strong opponent of quartering. *(National Archives, Department of State)*

bearing arms shall be compelled to render military service in person."

Elbridge Gerry of Massachusetts objected to the last part of Madison's draft. He was worried about excusing people on the basis of religion. Under Madison's amendment, Gerry claimed, a president who did not like a particular religious group might simply determine that the members of that given religion could not serve in the militia. A group of delegates proposed adding the phrase "for the common defense." That move was defeated. Some Pennsylvanian anti-Federalists favored a different version: "The people have a right to bear arms for the defense of themselves and their own state, or the United States, or for the purpose of killing game." Pennsylvania's draft was also rejected. The final version of the Second Amendment passed as follows: "A well regulated Militia, being necessary to the security of a free State, the right of the people to keep and bear Arms shall not be infringed."

The argument about the Third Amendment centered on the difference between quartering in peace and in wartime. Everyone favored banning forced quartering during peacetime, but some delegates thought that quartering might be necessary during times of national emergency. Thomas Sumter of South Carolina proposed a complete ban: "No soldier shall be quartered in any house without the consent of the owner." Roger Sherman of Connecticut objected to Sumter's suggestion. An individual citizen, said Sherman, should not be allowed to damage the safety of the public. Sometimes soldiers might need to be placed in private homes. Gerry, representing Massachusetts, suggested this version: "No soldier shall, in time of peace, be Quartered in any house, without the consent of the owner, nor in time of war but by a civil magistrate in a manner prescribed by law." Thomas Hartley of Pennsylvania worried that one civil magistrate might misuse this power. He wanted the legislature to decide that quartering was necessary. To this end, the Third Amendment was passed in this form: "No soldier shall, in time of peace be quartered in any house, without the consent of the Owner, nor in time of war but in a manner to be prescribed by law."

With the passage of the Bill of Rights, the Second and Third Amendments and eight others became basic rights of American citizens. In the two centuries since, quartering has seldom been a matter of concern. In modern times, however, the right to keep and bear arms has almost never been absent from the news.

4

The Second Amendment and Gun Control Laws

For about 150 years, only state and local laws determined who could legally buy, sell, carry, and use guns in the United States, and few Americans debated gun control on the federal level. As the 1920s dawned, concern about violent crime increased sharply. During this decade gangsters committed a number of well-publicized, bloody murders. After each incident, the debate about gun control heated up.

Citizens who wanted federal control of guns believed that state and local laws were not effective enough. They pointed out that criminals in a state with strict gun control laws could simply go to a different location to purchase a weapon or send for one by mail. Opponents of firearm regulation argued that criminals, by definition, break laws. Therefore, gangsters would probably not obey federal gun control laws, either. Following this logic, control laws would disarm only law-abiding citizens.

Opponents of gun control also argued that laws restricting firearms were not constitutional. The Second Amendment, they said, protected individual Americans' right to keep and bear arms. People who supported gun control laws, on the other hand, viewed the Second Amendment differently. They saw the right to keep and bear arms as belonging to the state militias, not to individual citizens.

FEDERAL GUN CONTROL LAWS

By the end of the 1920s, the nation had its first federal gun control law. In the years since, Congress has passed about a dozen more laws regulating the manufacture, transport, sale, possession, and

THE ROARING TWENTIES
AND GUN CONTROL

In 1921, former brigadier general John T. Thompson invented a new type of gun. Thompson's creation, nicknamed the "tommy gun," was capable of firing 800 bullets a minute. The tommy gun was advertised as a tool for the police—an "antibandit gun that would stop getaway cars in their tracks"—but it soon became popular with violent criminals. One newspaper writer condemned the new weapon, calling it "nothing less than a diabolical [devilish] engine of death." The writer went on to say that with a tommy gun, one criminal could "stand off a whole platoon of policemen."

In the early 1920s, the tommy gun was used in a number of famous crimes. During the same period, mail order sales of cheap pistols increased greatly. Some Americans believed that the easy availability of these dangerous weapons was at least partly to blame for the rising violence of the "Roaring Twenties." Others believed that Prohibition, not guns, was to blame. Prohibition was a national ban on alcoholic beverages according to a constitutional amendment (the Eighteenth Amendment) that took effect in 1920 and was repealed in 1933. Critics believed that barring alcohol encouraged criminal activity.

This World War II–era soldier holds four tommy guns. *(Franklin Delano Roosevelt Library)*

use of firearms. Each law has been praised by some citizens and condemned by others.

Miller Act (1927)

John Miller, a representative from Washington State, proposed a law banning the use of the U.S. postal system to send pistols and other small firearms to private citizens across state lines. Miller said that his bill would decrease crime by limiting the sale of pistols, which he called the "pet of the highway man, of the robber, and

> "I do not believe this bill would stop a single thug or a single bootlegger or a single murderer from carrying firearms unlawfully."
>
> —*Representative Thomas Blanton of Texas during the 1924 debate in Congress about a bill to ban the shipment of handguns through the mail*

After a gun battle with the police in 1931, the bodies of gangsters lie next to a bullet-riddled taxi. *(National Archives, U.S. Information Agency)*

the thief." Many members of Congress, particularly those from the South and the West, attacked the bill. In February 1927, it nonetheless became law: The Mailing of Firearms Act, or Miller Act, was the first nationwide law regarding firearms. The Miller Act had almost no effect on the sale of guns; manufacturers simply shipped firearms by private carriers.

National Firearms Act (1934)

The National Firearms Act of 1934 was intended to block the use of submachine guns, that is, tommy guns and other weapons that fire a large number of bullets in a very short time. It also attempted to control sawed-off shotguns, whose shortened barrels could be easily hidden. The act required manufacturers, importers, and sellers to register and keep track of these weapons and to pay a tax. Buyers, who also paid a high tax, were to be fingerprinted and investigated before the purchase could be completed. This act also outlawed the possession of bombs, missiles, grenades, and silencers by private citizens.

Federal Firearms Act (1938)

During the 1930s, public opinion in favor of gun registration grew. A poll taken in 1935 found that 84 percent of Americans thought that "all owners of pistols and revolvers should be required to register with the federal government." Also, President Franklin Roosevelt strongly backed this form of gun control. Many groups, including the National Rifle Association (NRA), the Sporting Arms and Ammunition Manufacturers Association, and local gun clubs opposed firearms registration.

> "Show me a man who does not want his gun registered and I will show you a man who should not have a gun."
>
> —Homer Cummings, attorney general during the administration of President Franklin Roosevelt, commenting on the Federal Firearms Act of 1938

INTERSTATE COMMERCE AND GUN CONTROL

The Constitution gives Congress the power to regulate interstate and international commerce, or trade. Federal laws regulating firearms are usually founded on Congress's commerce power. Federal firearm laws, therefore, apply only to weapons that cross state or national borders at some point; for example, the parts or finished weapons have been shipped to a buyer or manufacturer in another state or country. Almost all guns fall in this category, so almost all are affected by federal laws.

For several years, Senator Royal Copeland of New York proposed a number of strict laws on registration, but none gathered the necessary support. A weaker bill without a registration requirement, the Federal Firearm Act, was voted into law in 1938. The Federal Firearms Act required manufacturers of firearms and anyone who shipped firearms across state or international borders to obtain a license from the federal government and to keep track of weapon sales. No firearms could be sold to people who did not have the permits required by their home state. No one convicted of a serious crime (a felony) was allowed to receive an interstate firearms shipment, and it was illegal to ship a gun with an erased or changed serial number.

Omnibus Crime Control and Safe Streets Act (1968)

In the 1960s, President John F. Kennedy, his brother Robert Kennedy, and the civil rights leader Reverend Martin Luther King, Jr., were assassinated. The public was horrified by these crimes, and

Reverend Martin Luther King, Jr. (third from left in the front row), and Robert Kennedy (fourth from left in the front row) were assassinated in 1968. *(Abbie Rowe, National Park Service/John Fitzgerald Kennedy Library, Boston)*

pressure for tighter gun control laws increased. In fact, shortly after President Kennedy's death, 17 separate federal gun control bills were introduced in Congress. (At the state government level, 170 bills were proposed.)

The Omnibus Crime Control and Safe Streets Act, also known as the Gun Control Act, was passed in 1968. This law banned interstate shipment of pistols and revolvers to individuals. No one was allowed to buy a handgun outside his or her home state. When President Lyndon Johnson signed the bill into law, he commented that it was only a partial solution to the problem of gun violence; rifles and shotguns were not covered at all under the act. Johnson promised to seek stronger gun control measures.

Gun Control Act of 1968

As promised, President Johnson pressed for additional gun laws, and in October 1968, the Gun Control Act of 1968 was passed. This law, together with the Omnibus Crime Control and Safe Streets Act, replaced the 1938 Federal Firearms Act. The Gun Control Act of 1968 raised license fees and created stricter licensing rules for dealers and manufacturers who shipped guns or gun parts from one state to another or to another country. Military weapons and "Saturday night specials" (cheap handguns) could not be imported into the United States. Mentally disabled people and those convicted of serious crimes were not allowed to buy weapons. A minimum purchasing age of 21 for pistols and 18 for rifles and shotguns was established. If a federal crime was committed with a gun, the criminal was subject to additional jail time.

Law Enforcement Officers Protection Act (1986)

To protect themselves, police officers often wear bulletproof vests. However, certain types of bullets, nicknamed "armor-piercing bullets," can pass through these vests and kill or wound the wearer. The Law Enforcement Officers Protection Act of 1986 bans the manufacture, importing, sale, and use of some brands of this sort of ammunition. Critics of this law said that too many types of armor-piercing bullets were still legal and pointed out that ammunition for rifles was not covered by the law.

Firearms Owners' Protection Act (1986)

As early as 1981, a senate committee began hearings about the possibility of removing federal gun controls or making them less strict. Nothing happened until 1985, when Senator James A. McClure of Idaho introduced a new gun law intended to replace the Gun Control Act of 1968.

The Firearms Owners' Protection Act became law in 1986. According to this law, it was legal to buy or sell rifles and shotguns, but not handguns, across state lines as long as the buyers' and sellers' states did not prohibit the sale. Ammunition dealers no longer needed to keep records tracking the purchase of bullets. The law also made it easier for private individuals to sell weapons. Penalties for crimes committed with guns were increased.

A separate law, passed about a month later, tightened some licensing and record-keeping rules for guns. Pro–gun control people still felt that the nation's weapons laws were not nearly strict enough.

Undetectable Firearms Act (1988)

The Undetectable Firearms Act of 1988 made it illegal to make, import, or sell guns that cannot be detected by ordinary security screening machines such as the ones used in airports. This law was mainly intended to curb plastic guns, which may be able to slip by metal detectors.

THE GUN SHOW ISSUE

One part of the Firearm Owners' Protection Act attracted much debate. The law eased the rules for licensing and allowed sellers without federal licenses to operate at gun shows. Gun shows are temporary markets, often held on the weekends, where everything from the newest models to antique and used weapons are sold. Critics charge that many criminals, drawn by the lack of rules, buy their guns at these shows. Others say that gun shows satisfy a need for law-abiding gun purchasers who may live far from the nearest gun shop.

Executive Orders on Assault Weapons (1989, 1998)

In January 1989, a man named Patrick Purdy sprayed bullets over a children's playground in Stockton, California. His weapons were an AK-47 assault rifle and a pistol. An assault rifle is a semiautomatic weapon. Five children were killed; 33 children and one teacher were wounded. Purdy then shot himself. The Stockton shooting horrified Americans. In a poll taken shortly after, 75 percent said that the federal government should ban semiautomatic rifles such as the AK-47. President George H. W. Bush issued an executive order banning the importing of AK-47s and some other types of semiautomatic weapons. The order was challenged in court but was declared constitutional. In 1998, President Bill Clinton also issued an executive order banning military-style assault rifles. Neither order applied to assault weapons manufactured in the United States. (Assault weapons are also regulated by the Violent Crime Control and Law Enforcement Act of 1994.)

> "I don't believe in taking away the right of the citizen to own a gun for sports, hunting, or their own personal defense. But I do not believe that an AK-47, a machine gun, is a sporting weapon."
>
> —*former President Ronald Reagan, commenting on a 1989 executive order banning some types of assault weapons*

Gun Free School Zones Act and the Gun-Free Schools Act (1990, 1995)

The Gun Free School Zones Act of 1990 banned the possession of firearms in a school zone, which is made up of the school itself and everything within 1,000 feet of school property. The Gun

Today guns are banned in schools. These World War II–era high school students are learning marksmanship in their school. *(Franklin Delano Roosevelt Library)*

Free School Zones Act was based on the power of Congress to set rules for commerce, or trade, between states. Lawmakers who supported this law claimed that violent crime hurt business, or commerce, by distracting students from their education. This law was challenged in court and overturned by the Supreme Court.

Congress then rewrote the law, calling it the Gun-Free Schools Act. This act, which was passed in 1995, also banned guns from schools and school zones. The Gun-Free Schools Act specified that the ban applied only to guns that had been shipped across state lines. In this way, lawmakers were able to base the gun law on their power to regulate interstate commerce. According to the Gun-Free Schools Act, school officials must suspend for one year any student who brings a gun to school or risk the loss of federal education aid.

Brady Handgun Violence Prevention Act (1993)

James Brady was President Ronald Reagan's press secretary. On March 30, 1981, Brady was walking with the president when John Hinckley opened fire on both of them. Hinckley, an unstable young man, had lied about his mental health when purchasing his weapon, a Saturday night special handgun he had bought at a pawn shop for $29. The president was wounded but recovered. Brady was paralyzed. Some time after the shooting, James Brady and his wife, Sarah, became gun control activists. The Brady Handgun Violence Prevention Act, often shortened to the Brady Bill, passed in 1993. The Brady Bill increased the fees that dealers pay for federal licenses. It required dealers to report multiple gun sales to law enforcement officials. The act also called for the establishment of a national computerized background check system and a five-day waiting period between the selection of a firearm and completion of the sale. With this system in place, gun buyers can be checked before their gun purchases are completed. People who have committed a serious crime, those under court order, anyone convicted of selling or using drugs, and mentally unstable individuals can be identified in the screening process and barred from buying guns.

Before the computerized system was set up, the Brady Bill called for local officers "to make a reasonable effort" to see that gun buyers met the legal requirements for gun ownership. Two sheriffs challenged the law, saying that the federal government could not require local officials to conduct background checks without pro-

THE BRADYS BEHIND THE BRADY BILL

James S. Brady was born in Centralia, Illinois, in 1940. He spent most of his life in public service, working for various government agencies. In January 1981, he was appointed White House press secretary by President Ronald Reagan. Only two months later, Brady accompanied his boss to an appearance at a Washington, D.C., hotel. A mentally unbalanced young man, John Hinckley, fired a gun at the president and his staff. Reagan was seriously wounded, though he recovered fully. Brady's head wound caused permanent damage.

Sarah, Brady's wife, had worked in education and for the Republican Party. After the shooting, the Bradys became active in the gun control movement. Sarah Brady chaired Handgun Control, Inc., in 1989. In 1991, she headed the Center to Prevent Handgun Violence, now renamed the Brady Center to Prevent Gun Violence. In 1993, President Bill Clinton signed a gun control bill that the Bradys had strongly supported. This law is sometimes called the Brady Bill in honor of James and Sarah Brady.

James and Sarah Brady work for stronger gun control laws. *(Brady Campaign to Prevent Gun Violence United with the Million Mom March)*

viding funds to pay for this work. The sheriffs won the case. The computerized system was ready soon after the case was decided.

Violent Crime Control and Law Enforcement Act (1994)

The Violent Crime Control and Law Enforcement Act barred juveniles from owning handguns. It outlawed for 10 years the manufacture, sale, and possession of 19 different types of semiautomatic weapons known as assault rifles. Some of the banned weapons include Uzis, AK-47s, and AR15s. The law also specified that magazines, or ammunition cartridges, could not contain more than 10 bullets each.

The Violent Crime Control and Law Enforcement Act did not apply to sporting rifles, and people who already owned assault weapons were allowed to keep them. The bill is due to expire in September 2004. President George W. Bush says he supports extending the assault weapons ban.

STATE GUN LAWS

In addition to federal laws, hundreds of state and local laws also regulate firearms. These regulations vary from state to state or from town to town. Some state laws are tougher than those passed by the

Supporters of stronger gun control laws would like to see all handguns equipped with child safety devices such as trigger locks. The gun in the foreground is equipped with a trigger lock. *(Peter Morgan/Reuters/Landov)*

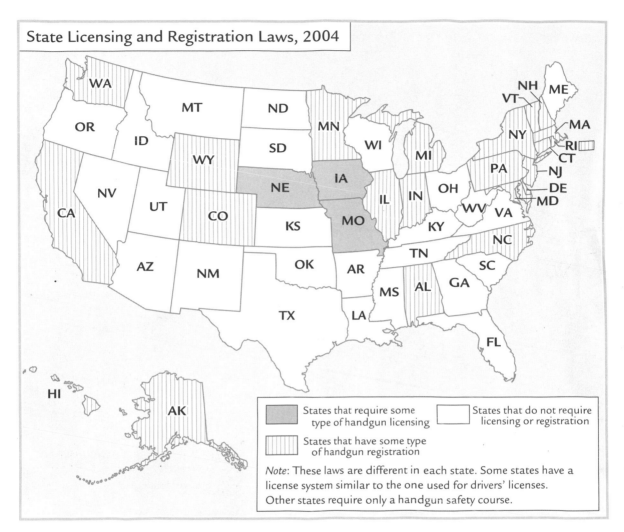

State Licensing and Registration Laws, 2004

Legend:
- States that require some type of handgun licensing
- States that have some type of handgun registration
- States that do not require licensing or registration

Note: These laws are different in each state. Some states have a license system similar to the one used for drivers' licenses. Other states require only a handgun safety course.

federal government. Everyone in the United States must follow federal laws. Gun owners or dealers must also follow the laws of the states in which they live or do business. In general, state gun laws address these issues:

- **Registration:** The law may require gun owners to register the serial numbers of their weapons with law enforcement officials.
- **Licensing:** The state may require a license to manufacture, buy, or sell firearms. Purchasers may also need a license.
- **Permit to Carry:** The state may regulate who is permitted to carry a weapon. Some states are very strict; the purchaser must show that he or she needs to carry a gun. In other

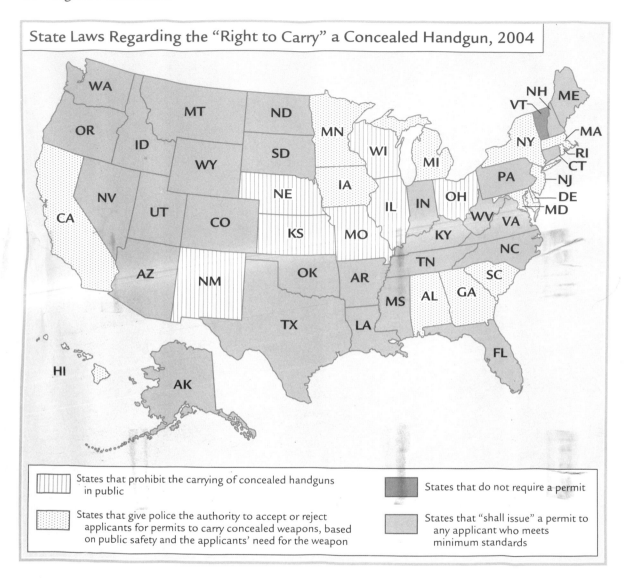

State Laws Regarding the "Right to Carry" a Concealed Handgun, 2004

States that prohibit the carrying of concealed handguns in public

States that give police the authority to accept or reject applicants for permits to carry concealed weapons, based on public safety and the applicants' need for the weapon

States that do not require a permit

States that "shall issue" a permit to any applicant who meets minimum standards

states citizens must be given a permit to carry a concealed handgun unless a particular reason—mental illness, age, or previous crimes, for example—bars the citizen from gun ownership. These states are often called "shall issue" states, because the government shall issue a permit to all those who apply except to those in restricted categories. Two states require no permit at all. Five states forbid concealed weapons entirely.

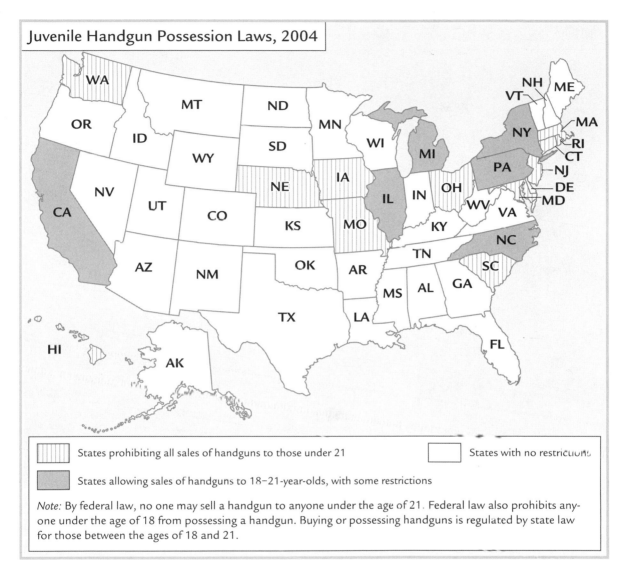

Juvenile Handgun Possession Laws, 2004

States prohibiting all sales of handguns to those under 21 | States with no restrictions

States allowing sales of handguns to 18–21-year-olds, with some restrictions

Note: By federal law, no one may sell a handgun to anyone under the age of 21. Federal law also prohibits any-one under the age of 18 from possessing a handgun. Buying or possessing handguns is regulated by state law for those between the ages of 18 and 21.

- **Storage:** Some state laws regulate how weapons must be stored when they are not in use—in a locked cabinet, for example.
- **Child Access:** Some state laws require that a weapon be kept out of the reach of children. Child access protection laws hold the adults legally responsible for the consequences if their chil-dren improperly gain access to a firearm. In a few states, deal-ers must offer to sell a trigger lock whenever a gun is purchased.

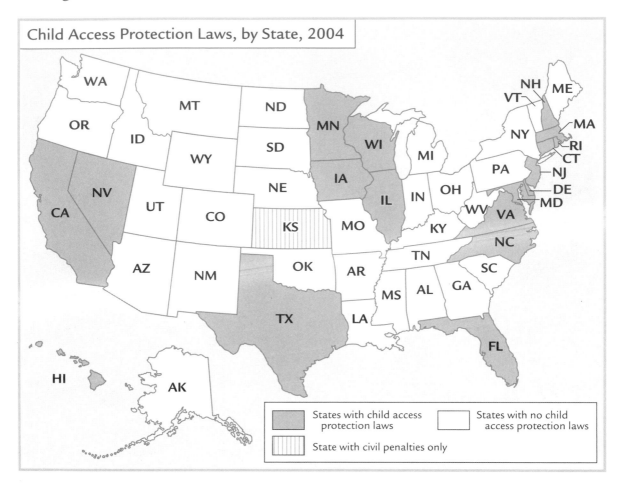

Child Access Protection Laws, by State, 2004

States with child access protection laws

State with civil penalties only

States with no child access protection laws

◆ **Special Restrictions:** State laws may set age limits or ban certain categories of people from gun ownership, such as mentally unstable people, those who have been convicted of serious crimes, and people judged dangerous to society.

5

The Second and Third Amendments in the Courts

An impressive white stone building in Washington, D.C., houses one-third of the U.S. government: the Supreme Court. The nine justices of the Court are appointed for life, and they are the highest legal authority in the nation. When they reach a decision, no further appeal is possible. One of the tasks of the Supreme Court of the United States is to interpret the U.S. Constitution, including the Bill of Rights. The Third Amendment has never been the subject of a Supreme Court case, though it was once addressed by a lower court. The Second Amendment, on the other hand, has been addressed by the Supreme Court many times.

HOW COURT CASES ARE NAMED

Court cases pit two sides against each other. In most Second Amendment cases, one side is the government agency responsible for enforcing the law. The government's side may be called by its location—"The Village of Morton Grove," for example—or by the name of the official in charge. Cases involving the federal government often use "United States" as the name of the government's side. The opposing side is the accused or convicted citizen or a gun owner who believes that the Second Amendment has been violated. The two sides are separated by the Latin word *versus*, which means "against." *Versus* is generally abbreviated as *v.* or sometimes as *vs.*

The Supreme Court rules on the constitutionality of many U.S. laws, including gun control regulations. *(National Archives)*

Laws passed by Congress and local governments may be challenged in the Supreme Court. When the Supreme Court accepts a case, the justices measure the law in question against the principles of the Constitution. They study the language of the Constitution itself, earlier court decisions, and English and American tradition. If the law is declared "unconstitutional," it must be taken off the books, and charges are dropped against anyone who was arrested for violating the law. If the law is judged acceptable, it is allowed to stand. The justices may decide not to hear a case because they see no constitutional question or because they believe that the lower court decision was correct.

The justices write an opinion for the cases they hear, explaining the reasons for their decision. Any justice who disagrees with the majority opinion may write a separate explanation. Justices who voted with the majority may also choose to write individual opinions. The opinions for each case are just as important as the verdict itself. The standards explained in an opinion are carefully studied by judges and lawyers around the country, who apply the principles of the law described in the majority opinion to cases in the lower courts. Lawmakers also study Supreme Court opinions to make sure that new laws do not violate the Constitution.

SUPREME COURT DECISIONS

The Supreme Court's rulings have not settled the debate about the meaning of "the right to keep and bear arms" granted by the Second Amendment. In fact, at times the same statement from an opinion has been used to support completely opposite viewpoints.

United States v. Cruikshank (1876)

The first Supreme Court case to deal directly with the Second Amendment took place in 1876. The local authorities arrested William J. Cruikshank and 95 other white citizens of the state of Louisiana after they had taken part in a violent attack on African Americans. Cruikshank and the other whites were accused of trying to prevent Levi Nelson and Alexander Tillman, two black citizens, from exercising their constitutional rights, including the right to vote. According to court papers, Cruikshank and his fellow defendants were also charged with attempting to "prevent the exercise . . . of the 'right to keep and bear arms for a lawful purpose'" by the two African Americans.

The Court ruled in favor of Cruikshank. In the opinion accompanying the case, the Court stated that the Second Amendment has only one function: to limit the powers of the national government. It does not restrict the powers of the states, nor does the Second Amendment apply to citizens whose rights have been violated by private individuals. It protects citizens from the federal government, but not from one another.

One phrase in the *United States v. Cruikshank* opinion has been the subject of much discussion. The Court wrote that the right to keep and bear arms is not "dependent" upon the Constitution "for its existence." Those who oppose gun control see this statement as

"Bearing arms for a lawful purpose . . . is not a right granted by the Constitution."

—*Supreme Court majority opinion in* United States v. Cruikshank, *1876*

proof that the right to bear arms is so basic that it existed even before there was a U.S. government to guarantee it. Pro–gun control groups argue that this statement is irrelevant because the right to bear arms belongs to state militias, not to individuals. They emphasize the main point of the Court's decision: that the Second Amendment does nothing more than limit the power of the federal government.

Presser v. State of Illinois (1886)

Herman Presser was a German immigrant who lived in Chicago in the late 19th century. Presser was a member of a German society whose name, translated into English, was "the Learning and Defense Club." According to its charter, the club aimed to improve "the mental and bodily condition of its members so as to qualify them for the duties of citizens of a republic." Society members studied U.S. laws and politics and practiced "military and gymnastic exercises."

On September 24, 1879, Presser led the members of his society, some 400 men, through the streets of Chicago. Presser rode on horseback, in uniform, carrying a cavalry sword. His "troops," the society members, were armed with rifles. Presser was arrested and charged with violating an Illinois State law forbidding "bodies of men to associate together as military organizations, or to drill or parade with arms in cities and towns unless authorized by law." The arrest warrant noted that Presser and his society members were not part of the "organized militia of the state, nor part of the troops of the United States" and that they had "no license from the governor of Illinois to drill or parade." Presser pleaded not guilty. He was convicted and fined $10 for his crime. He appealed his case all the way to the Supreme Court, claiming among other things that the Illinois law had violated his Second Amendment right to bear arms.

Presser lost his case. According to the Supreme Court opinion, the Second Amendment protects the rights of the states, ensuring that the federal government does not disarm state militias. The Second Amendment, said the Court, does not limit the power of the state to regulate military associations and parades by armed private soldiers; therefore, the Illinois State law was not unconstitutional. The opinion also stated that state and federal laws may regulate when and in what manner individuals may possess firearms.

Some Supreme Court cases have ruled that the right to bear arms is a collective right, allowing the government "its rightful resource for maintaining public security." *(NARA, Office of Emergency Management)*

"The states cannot . . . prohibit the people from keeping and bearing arms, so as to deprive [take away from] the United States of their rightful resource for maintaining the public security."

—*Supreme Court majority opinion in* Presser v. State of Illinois, *1886*

However, a separate statement from the Court also explained that "all citizens capable of bearing arms" make up the militia or a reserve militia of the United States or of individual states. The Court said that neither the states nor the federal government may limit guns so severely that the militia can no longer exist. Since the opinion clearly includes "all citizens capable of bearing arms" in the definition of the militia, some see the opinion as supporting an individual's right to gun ownership.

Miller v. Texas (1894)

On July 23, 1892, a Texan named Franklin P. Miller was found guilty of murdering a police officer who had tried to arrest Miller for carrying an unlicensed handgun. Miller was sentenced to death. He appealed the verdict, claiming that his arrest was based partly on the fact that he had been carrying a pistol. Miller claimed that the Texas law regulating firearms was unconstitutional because it violated his Second Amendment right to keep and bear arms. Miller hoped that the case against him would be weakened enough to overturn his murder conviction.

The Supreme Court ruled against Franklin Miller. The Court said that Miller should have raised the issue of the Second Amendment during his trial, not just at the Supreme Court level. Furthermore, the Court ruled that Miller's objection to the Texas law was incorrect, because, wrote the Court, "it is well settled that the restrictions of [the Second Amendment] operate only on federal power, and have no reference whatever to proceedings in state courts." In other words, the Second Amendment is only a protection from the power of the federal government, not from the laws of a particular state.

United States v. Miller (1939)

In 1934, Congress passed the National Firearms Act, the first federal law regulating possession of firearms. The National Firearms Act applied to machine guns and "sawed-off shotguns," rifles with shortened barrels. The act required anyone taking these types of firearms across state lines to register, pay a $200 tax, and receive an official stamp for each weapon.

The case known as *United States v. Miller* began in 1939, when Jack Miller and Frank Layton were arrested and charged with violating the National Firearms Act. According to court documents, the pair had carried an unregistered weapon, a "double barrel 12 gauge Stevens shotgun with a barrel less than 18 inches in length" from Claremore, Oklahoma, to Siloam Springs, Arkansas. The charges against Miller and Layton stated that they did not have in their possession a stamped "written order" for their sawed-off shotgun while crossing state lines and that they had therefore violated "the peace and dignity of the United States" by breaking the law.

Miller and Layton's defense was that the National Firearms Act was unconstitutional. They claimed that the act illegally limited their right to bear arms by placing an improper tax on sawed-off shotguns. A federal district court in Arkansas agreed with Miller and Layton and ordered that the charges against the men be dropped. However, the federal government continued to press its case against the two men.

By the time the case reached the Supreme Court, Miller and Layton were no longer part of it: Before the hearing, Miller had been murdered, and Layton had disappeared. The government's lawyers argued alone, claiming that the National Firearms Act was constitutional. The Supreme Court agreed with the government.

The Court's opinion in *United States v. Miller* discussed the role of the militia in the American colonies and in the states during the early decades of U.S. history. The Court noted that "in all the colonies, as in England, the militia system was based on . . . the general obligation of all adult male inhabitants to possess arms, and, with certain exceptions, to cooperate in the work of defense." However, the Court stated, there was no evidence "tending to show that possession or use of a 'shotgun having a barrel of less than 18 inches in length' . . . has some reasonable relationship to the preservation or efficiency of a well regulated militia." Therefore, wrote the Court, "We cannot say that the Second Amendment guarantees the right to keep and bear" such a weapon. In other words, because militia members do not use them, the Second Amendment does not conflict with a law regulating sawed-off shotguns.

People who support gun control laws and people who oppose them both find evidence for their points of view in *United States v. Miller.* Supporters of gun control laws point to the fact that the Court connected the right to bear arms with the existence of a militia. As they interpret the Court's ruling, the U.S. Constitution gives the right to bear arms only to organized groups of soldiers controlled by state officials. To prove that this viewpoint is correct, supporters of gun control laws turn to one section of the opinion, which discusses the U.S. Constitution's division of rights and responsibilities concerning militias. The opinion in *United States v. Miller* stated that the Second Amendment "must be interpreted and applied with . . . [the establishment and maintenance of the Militia] in view."

People who do not support gun control laws, on the other hand, focus on the fact that Miller and Layton were private individuals. The Court did not ask, "Are Miller and Layton militias?" or "Are Miller and Layton state governments?" If the Court truly wanted to link the right to bear arms only to state governments and militias, these two questions would have been enough to settle the case. Instead, the Court considered whether the law applied to a particular type of weapon (the sawed-off shotgun), not whether an individual American has the right to possess a gun. Opponents of gun control laws also point out that the Supreme Court did not discuss Layton's and Miller's right to bear arms, just the right to bear an unregistered weapon not associated with militia duty.

Lewis v. United States (1980)

The Omnibus Crime Control and Safe Streets Act of 1968 banned any person who had been convicted of a serious crime—a felony, in legal terms—from possessing a firearm. In 1961, a Florida State court found George Calvin Lewis guilty of breaking and entering, and he served time in prison. In January 1977, Lewis was arrested for possessing a firearm. During his trial, Lewis claimed that he had a right to possess the firearm because his felony conviction was flawed: He had not been represented by a lawyer in the 1961 breaking-and-entering case. The state court rejected Lewis's argument.

When the case reached the Supreme Court in 1980, the justices ruled against Lewis. The Court pointed out that Lewis could have challenged his 1961 conviction by asking for a new trial, this time with a jury. Lewis could also have asked for a pardon or for special permission to own a gun. Lewis did neither. Moreover, the Court recognized that the Omnibus Crime Control and Safe Streets Act was clearly designed to keep firearms out of the hands of people

"Congress sought . . . to keep guns out of the hands of those who have demonstrated that 'they may not be trusted to possess a firearm without becoming a threat to society.'"

—*Supreme Court majority opinion in* Lewis v. U.S., *1980, quoting from statements made in Congress when the 1968 gun control bill was debated*

who were likely to be dangerous. The opinion went on to say that denying guns to a convicted criminal, even a criminal who did not have a lawyer during his or her trial, was "rational."

United States v. Lopez (1995)

On March 10, 1992, Alfonso Lopez, Jr., took a gun and five bullets with him to his school in San Antonio, Texas. School officials received an anonymous tip and asked Lopez whether he was carrying a weapon. Lopez admitted that he had a gun, and he was arrested and charged with violating the Gun Free School Zones Act of 1990, which made it a federal offense "for any individual knowingly to possess a firearm at a place that the individual knows . . . is a school zone." Congress passed the Gun Free School Zones Act using its authority to regulate interstate commerce, or trade. The reasoning was that violent or dangerous schools do not properly educate young Americans, who therefore cannot take part in commerce, or business, upon graduation. Also, violent crime costs money—medical expenses, insurance premiums, police salaries—and money is certainly related to the nation's economy and therefore to commerce.

When the case reached the Supreme Court, the justices ruled that the Gun Free School Zones Act was unconstitutional because education is *not* commerce. Congress overreached in passing the act, said the justices, because the connection between education and future careers in business was too slight. Furthermore, the fact that violent crime has an impact on commerce is not enough to justify banning guns in schools. Congress reacted to the Court's judgment by passing a new law, the Gun-Free Schools Act, which banned guns that had been bought or sold in interstate commerce from schools. The new law also called for a one-year expulsion for any student who brought a firearm to school. Schools choosing not to follow this expulsion policy risked losing federal aid.

Printz v. United States (1997)

The Brady Handgun Violence Prevention Act of 1993 (Brady Bill) is a gun control law passed after the attempted assassination of President Ronald Reagan and the wounding of his press secretary James Brady in 1981. The law called for a national computerized list to allow for speedy background checks on gun purchasers. Until the

President Bill Clinton signs the Brady Bill in the presence of former White House press secretary James Brady. *(Gary Hershom/Reuters/Landov)*

computer program was set up, local law enforcement officials were supposed to make background checks. Two sheriffs—Jay Printz of Ravalli County, Montana, and Richard Mack of Graham County, Arizona—challenged the law in court. They claimed that Congress had no right to demand work from local police without providing funding. The Supreme Court ruled in favor of the sheriffs. Shortly after the decision, the computer program was ready, and background checks by sheriffs were no longer an issue.

United States v. Bean (2002)

Thomas Lamar Bean, a gun dealer, crossed the border from the United States into Mexico in 2001 with 200 rounds of ammunition in his car. Mexican authorities arrested Bean for illegally importing ammunition; he was convicted and sentenced to jail. Because he had been found guilty of a serious crime, Bean was no longer permitted by U.S. law to possess or distribute firearms and ammunition.

Bean applied to the federal agency that regulates firearms, the Bureau of Alcohol, Tobacco, and Firearms (ATF) for an exception. After all, his livelihood was threatened by his inability to handle guns legally. The ATF responded that since 1992, it was prohibited from granting such requests by an act of Congress. Bean next turned to the courts. A lower court gave Bean the exception he requested. However, the Supreme Court ruled in 2002 that only the ATF, not the courts, could restore Bean's right to possess firearms.

LOWER COURT DECISIONS

One level under the Supreme Court are the federal courts of appeal. There are 13 of these courts, each covering a large area called a "circuit." The federal court system also includes other, lower courts. All these courts have made important rulings on the Second Amendment.

United States v. Tot (1942)

On September 22, 1938, federal officers entered the home of Frank Tot of Newark, New Jersey, in search of cigarettes stolen from an interstate shipment. They found a .32-caliber Colt automatic pistol. Tot had previously been arrested and convicted of a violent crime,

---

HOW COURT RULINGS ARE APPLIED

Not every court decision applies to the entire United States, as Supreme Court decisions do. The decisions of the circuit court judges apply only to their area, not to the other circuits; in fact, the decisions in one circuit may be very different from those of another circuit, particularly on controversial issues such as gun control. In recent years, for example, the Fifth Circuit and the Ninth Circuit have taken completely opposite positions on the meaning of the Second Amendment.

"Weapon bearing was never treated as anything like an absolute right by the common law."

—*from the majority opinion, U.S. Court of Appeals for the Third Circuit, in* United States v. Tot, *1942*

so the agents charged him with violating the Federal Firearms Act of 1934, which barred violent criminals from possessing firearms that had been transported in interstate or foreign commerce.

Tot appealed his conviction, claiming that several of his rights had been violated, including his Second Amendment rights. The appeals court for the Third Circuit did not accept Tot's arguments regarding the right to keep and bear arms. The court's opinion stated that the Second Amendment "was not adopted with individual rights in mind, but as a protection for the States in the maintenance of their militia organizations." The court quoted from the Supreme Court's 1939 decision in *United States v. Miller* to support its reasoning. Tot had no right to a weapon, said the circuit court, because the Firearms Act was "for the protection of society against violent men armed with dangerous weapons."

Quilici v. Village of Morton Grove (1983)

On June 8, 1981, the village of Morton Grove, Illinois, passed Ordinance 81-11, a local law prohibiting the possession of a handgun within the village borders. Exceptions to this ban included the police, military personnel, prison officials, and licensed gun collectors and gun clubs. The ordinance required citizens who already owned handguns to turn in the weapons to the police or risk breaking the law.

Several residents of Morton Grove, including Victor D. Quilici, challenged Morton Grove's law in state court, claiming that their Second Amendment rights had been denied by Ordinance 81-11. Quilici and those who joined in his lawsuit based their case on a section of the Illinois State constitution that says, "Subject only to police power, the right of the individual citizen to keep and bear arms shall not be infringed [violated]."

Quilici v. Village of Morton Grove went through the court system and reached the Supreme Court in 1983. The Supreme Court justices, without comment, refused to hear it. Therefore, the judgment of the lower court, the U.S. Court of Appeals for the Seventh Circuit, stands. In its opinion, the circuit court ruled that the Morton Grove's Ordinance 81-11 did not violate the right to keep and bear arms given in either the Illinois constitution or the U.S. Constitution.

Considering the state constitution first, the circuit court opinion stated that the Illinois State constitution's "plain language

KENNESAW, GEORGIA

Shortly after Morton Grove, Illinois, banned handguns, a town in Georgia took the opposite approach. Kennesaw, Georgia, passed a law in 1982 stating that "every head of household . . . is required to maintain a firearm, together with ammunition" unless the householder was a criminal or a physically or mentally disabled person. Residents who objected to the law on religious grounds were also excused from gun ownership. The town said the law was "to provide for the civil defense of the City of Kennesaw . . . and [to] protect the safety, security, and general welfare of the City and its inhabitants." The law changed little in Kennesaw, as most residents already owned firearms.

grants only the right to keep and bear arms, not handguns." Homeowners in Morton Grove might, for example, own rifles or shotguns without violating Ordinance 81-11. The opinion quoted from the debate that took place when the Illinois constitution was being written. The comments, the circuit court said, clearly showed that the delegates knew that "local governments might exercise their police power to restrict, or prohibit, the right to keep and bear handguns." The opinion continued, "There is no right under the Illinois Constitution to possess a handgun. . . . Accordingly, Morton Grove may exercise its police power to prohibit handguns even though this prohibition interferes with an individual's liberty or property."

Next, the circuit court turned to the U.S. Constitution. The court quoted from *Presser v. State of Illinois* (1886), in which the Supreme Court ruled that the Second Amendment restricts only the federal government and permits states to regulate the use and possession of firearms. The federal circuit court emphasized that the right to bear arms is firmly linked to the preservation of a militia, not to individual possession of handguns.

Emerson v. United States (1999)

On August 28, 1998, Sacha Emerson filed for divorce in Tom Green County, Texas. Her petition requested that the court protect her from her husband, Timothy Joe Emerson, who had pointed a gun

> "All of the evidence indicates that the Second Amendment, like other parts of the Bill of Rights, applies to and protects individual Americans."
>
> —from the majority opinion, U.S. Court of Appeals for the Fifth Circuit, in Emerson v. United States, 1999

at Sacha and her daughter when they went to his office to pick up some insurance papers. Sacha's petition also alleged that Emerson had told an employee that he owned an AK-47 (an assault rifle) and that he planned to pay a visit to his wife's new boyfriend. According to court papers, Emerson himself told a police officer that if any of his wife's friends set foot on his property, they would "be found dead in the parking lot."

In response to Sacha's request, the court issued a restraining order, a legal document that barred Emerson from "threatening . . . in person, by telephone, or in writing to take unlawful action against any person" and threatening or "intentionally, knowingly, or recklessly causing bodily injury" to his wife or child.

On November 16, 1998, Emerson was arrested because, according to the police, he "unlawfully possessed . . . a firearm, a Beretta pistol" while he was subject to the restraining order. The police viewpoint was that Emerson's possession of a gun was a threat to his family. Emerson challenged the arrest, claiming his Second Amendment rights.

The case reached the appeals court for the Fifth Circuit in 1999. The court ruled that Emerson did not have a right to own a Beretta or any other firearm while he was under a restraining order. In an 80-page document, the court's opinion traced the right to keep and bear arms from colonial days through modern Supreme Court cases. The court's belief was that Emerson could be prohibited from owning a weapon because of his previous conduct toward his wife and because of the restraining order. However, the judges took pains to explain that the Second Amendment is, in their opinion, an individual right that may be limited only for very good reason and in a very limited way.

Gun control supporters praised the Emerson case for reaching the right conclusion, but they criticized the portion of the opinion that established an individual's right to keep and bear arms. The Supreme Court was asked to hear the case, but they refused, so the circuit court's decision stands.

Silveira v. Lockyer (2002)

In 1999, the state of California changed its gun control laws to limit even more strictly than before the possession, use, and sale of assault weapons. Assault weapons are capable of firing a large number of bullets in a short period of time and had been used in several high-profile shootings in the state and elsewhere. Sean Silveira and a number of other Californians who owned assault weapons or who wished to buy them challenged the new law as infringing on their Second Amendment rights.

When the case reached the Ninth Circuit court, the Second Amendment claim made by Silveira was firmly rejected. The opinion made many references to the Fifth Circuit's 1999 decision in *Emerson v. United States* and disagreed with almost everything in the *Emerson* opinion. According to the Ninth Circuit, "the Second Amendment does not confer [give] an individual right to own or possess arms." Like the Fifth Circuit, the Ninth Circuit appeals court examined the history of the Second Amendment's adoption and discussed the language of the amendment itself. However, the Ninth Circuit came to the opposite conclusion. The Ninth Circuit court wrote that the most believable interpretation of the amendment is that it "seeks to ensure the existence of effective state militias in which the people may exercise their right to bear arms, and forbids the federal government to interfere with such exercise."

GUN MANUFACTURER SUITS

In recent years, more than two dozen states, cities, and local governments have sued gun manufacturers, claiming that the companies are responsible for injury or death caused by their products. Additional lawsuits have been brought by organizations and individuals. Most of the lawsuits revolve around injuries related to violent crime. Dozens of lawsuits have yet to be decided. Of those that have been decided, the vast majority of the suits have been won by the gun manufacturers.

Regardless of the outcome, these lawsuits have had an effect on the firearms industry. Defending business practices in court is very expensive. To head off court action, some firearms companies have voluntarily created a code of conduct that attempts to increase safety and prevent misuse of their products. Congress is currently considering a bill protecting gun manufacturers from lawsuits of this kind.

NAACP v. Accusport Inc. et al (2003)

The National Association for the Advancement of Colored People (NAACP) sued more than 80 gun manufacturers in federal district court in Brooklyn, New York. The NAACP claimed that these companies were responsible for the deaths of many people of color because they allowed their products, handguns, to be marketed to criminals. The NAACP relied on statistics showing that people of color were more likely than others to be the target of gun violence. The NAACP also claimed that it was harmed because its members were prohibited from attending meetings because of fear of gun violence.

The judge ruled against the NAACP, stating that the NAACP had failed to show that the organization had suffered more harm than the general public, a condition required by New York law. In his opinion, however, the judge criticized the gun industry, saying that the gun manufacturers were "responsible for the creation of a public nuisance." The judge also wrote that the companies, through voluntary changes in marketing and sales practices, could easily limit gun violence.

THE SECOND AMENDMENT IN STATE COURTS

Many state court cases refer to the state constitutional guarantees of the right to keep and bear arms, which are given by 38 of the 50 U.S. states. Some of the state decisions have supported the militia, or collective rights, view of the Second Amendment, and others have favored the individual rights interpretation. State court decisions apply only to the state in which they are made. Important cases include

> *State v. Buzzard (1842):* The Arkansas Supreme Court ruled that the sole purpose of the Second Amendment was to secure a well-regulated militia.
> *Salina v. Blaksley (1905):* In this Kansas case, the militia view was strongly upheld.
> *People v. Brown (1931):* The Michigan Supreme Court supported a ban on individual possession of blackjacks, bombs, and rockets, saying that "some arms . . . are too dangerous to be kept in a settled community by an individual . . . and have legitimate employment only by guards and police."

Schubert v. DeBard (1980): The Indiana Supreme Court ruled that citizens do not have to show that they need a gun in order to obtain a license for one. This case supports the individual rights view.

Oregon State v. Kessler (1980): Oregon police arrested a man for possessing two billy clubs. The Oregon Supreme Court ruled that citizens have the right to bear arms for their personal defense.

Kelley v. R.G. Industries (1985): The Court of Appeals of Maryland decided that manufacturers of Saturday night specials—cheap, easily hidden handguns—could be sued for damages if the guns they manufactured were used in the commission of a crime. The court held that such weapons are not generally useful for sport or target shooting and are marketed to appeal to the criminal market.

Richardson v. Holland (1987): The Court of Appeals of Missouri ruled that gun manufacturers are not legally responsible for the misuse of their products.

THE THIRD AMENDMENT CASE

The right not to quarter troops in one's home was fiercely defended in colonial America, but in the history of the United States, it has been the subject of only one court case. In 1982, prison guards in New York State went on strike. The governor, Hugh Carey, ordered the state's National Guard to take over the strikers' duties. He quartered the troops in the state-owned residences of the striking guards. Two prison guards sued for violation of their Third Amendment rights, in *Englbom v. Carey.*

The U.S. Court of Appeals for the Second Circuit concluded that the prison guards, while not owning their residences, clearly viewed the residences as their homes. Quartering the National Guard in those residences, therefore, amounted to an offense against the guards' "expectation of privacy," which all citizens are entitled to. The court ruled in favor of the guards.

> "The Third Amendment was designed to assure a fundamental [basic] right to privacy."
>
> —*from the majority opinion, U.S. Court of Appeals for the Second Circuit, in* Englbom v. Carey, 1982

6

~~~~

Guns in the
United States Today

A police pistol, a hunting rifle, a handgun in a bedside drawer, a firearm drawn in a robbery, an assault rifle aimed at a target—these are snapshots of gun use in the United States today. As they have been since colonial times, firearms are part of the American way of life. They are also part of America's vision of itself. Countless movies, video games, and television shows feature the brave cowboy, the dangerous gunslinger, the heroic law officer, or the trigger-happy mobster.

Everyone knows that there are many guns in the United States, but no one knows the exact number. Criminals often obtain firearms illegally, and law enforcement officials have solid statistics only for weapons used in a crime. But it is hard to count even legally purchased guns. Many states require the registration of guns, especially handguns, but no nationwide system of tracking firearms exists. Most authorities believe that there are many more than 200 million guns in the United States. (The National Rifle Association's estimate is 240 million firearms.) Between 60 and 65 million of those weapons are handguns, according to the American Firearms Industry Web site. The American Firearms Industry Magazine also estimates that each year about 1 million new handguns are imported or are manufactured in the United States and not exported.

Of course, these new weapons are not the only guns in the United States. Firearms are very sturdy products; if a gun is properly maintained, it will work even after 100 years. In buying a new weapon, many gun owners are adding to their collection, not

TYPES OF GUNS AND AMMUNITION

Most guns burn an explosive mixture, gunpowder, to push ammunition at very high speed through a narrow tube, or barrel. Some firearms move ammunition into place after each shot. These weapons may be automatic, firing many bullets with each squeeze of the trigger, or semiautomatic, firing only one bullet per squeeze.

Rifles and shotguns have long barrels. Rifles, which fire bullets, may be accurate at a range of hundreds of yards. Shotguns spray tiny balls called shot over a small area. Shotguns are not as accurate as rifles and are generally effective for targets less than 100 yards away.

Handgun barrels measure two to eight inches. One common type of handgun is a revolver, which feeds five or six bullets into the barrel from a small, round container that revolves, or turns, after each shot.

Millions of Americans hunt for sport and for food. This hunter on snowshoes carries a rifle. The photograph is from 1935. *(National Archives, Bureau of Indian Affairs)*

> "Encouragement of a proper hunting spirit, a proper love of sport . . . offers the best guarantee for the preservation of wild things."
>
> *—President Theodore Roosevelt*

replacing an older gun. The NRA reports that about 45 percent of American households have some sort of firearm, old or new. A statistical snapshot of guns in the United States at the beginning of the 21st century includes both legal and illegal uses.

LEGAL GUN USE
Hunting

The NRA estimates that more than 14 million Americans aged 16 and older hunt with firearms. For some, hunting is a practical activity; the animals supply meat and sometimes other valuable goods such as fur and hides. For others, hunting is a sport. Shooting the animal is not as important as the experience of being in

In many communities young people are taught to hunt or target shoot. In 1972, these boys practiced with their guns in Louisiana. *(National Archives, Environmental Protection Agency)*

OLYMPIC ACCURACY

Several Olympic events measure shooting skills, including competitions with air rifles, air pistols, and sports pistols. Perhaps the most unusual of these events is the biathlon, a combination of cross-country skiing and target shooting. Athletes ski around a course, dropping to the ground at certain points to fire at targets 50 meters away. Strength and endurance are part of the challenge; athletes cannot aim well if they are out of breath. One writer compared competing in the biathlon to running up a flight of stairs and then threading a needle. Points are given for speed and accuracy.

❧❦❧

the wilderness and participating in an activity that is as old as humanity itself.

In many areas of the United States, hunters must purchase a hunting license or permit to hunt game. Since 1937, hunters have also paid a tax on sporting firearms and ammunition. The money from this tax goes to a special fund that states may use to preserve wildlife and provide safety training to hunters. According to the NRA, which publishes a magazine entitled *American Hunter,* hunters and fishermen have contributed about $20 billion for wildlife conservation.

Target Shooting

Each year, most of the nation's 10,000 rifle and gun clubs sponsor target-shooting tournaments. The NRA, which registers and publicizes these events, estimates that hundreds of thousands of Americans compete annually. Shooters score points for accuracy by firing rifles, air rifles, and handguns at targets a specified distance away or within a limited time period. In some contests, participants fire at moving targets or from a particular shooting position. Olympic medals are offered for several types of target shooting.

Protection

Members of the U.S. armed forces and state national guards routinely learn how to maintain and shoot a variety of weapons. Police

"Many of today's handgunners can make shots that were unheard of years ago because of their advanced equipment and participation in today's demanding sports."

—*Thomas J. Griffin,* Lyman Pistol and Revolver Reloading Handbook, Second Edition, *1994*

and corrections officers, who guard prisoners, also carry firearms. Most law enforcement professionals use handguns. Special units such as antiterrorist forces or SWAT teams, which are called out only for the most dangerous situations, may be armed with rifles or assault weapons.

Some private citizens keep weapons for self-defense. Home-owners may store a handgun or a rifle in the house, as a protection against intruders. The constitutions of 44 states mention the right to bear arms, and some refer specifically to self-defense as well. Some states permit citizens to carry firearms outside the home to defend themselves or others in case a criminal threatens. Statistics showing how private citizens use guns for self-defense have been gathered by both sides in the gun control debate. Depending on

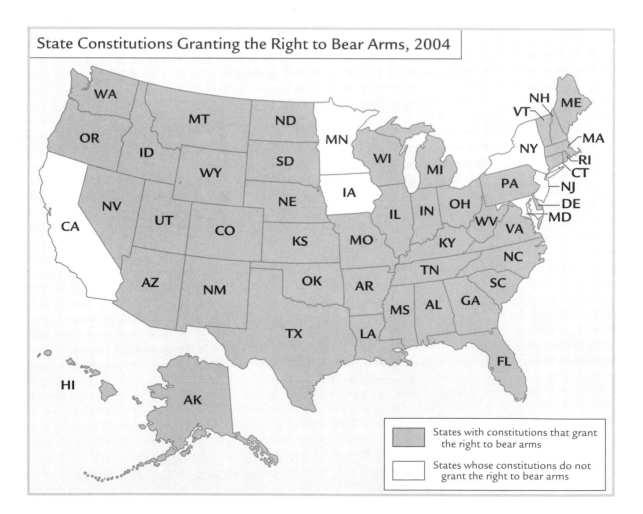

State Constitutions Granting the Right to Bear Arms, 2004

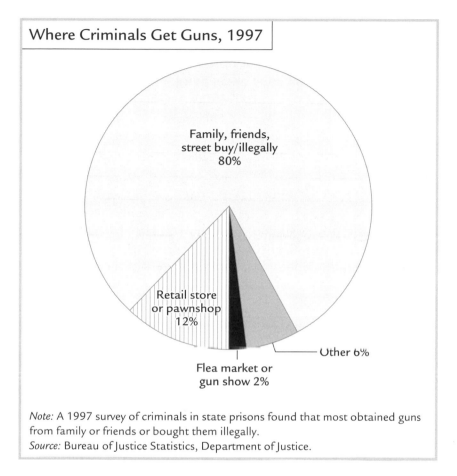

Where Criminals Get Guns, 1997

Family, friends,
street buy/illegally
80%

Retail store
or pawnshop
12%

Other 6%

Flea market or
gun show 2%

Note: A 1997 survey of criminals in state prisons found that most obtained guns from family or friends or bought them illegally.
Source: Bureau of Justice Statistics, Department of Justice.

how the results are interpreted, the number of successful self-defense incidents varies tremendously.

Supporters of gun control cite a 2003 report by the Brookings Institution, a Washington, D.C., think tank that studies public policy. The report concluded that communities with higher rates of gun ownership have a slightly higher number of burglaries. Specifically, the Brookings researchers found that a 10 percent increase in a county's gun ownership resulted in a 3–7 percent increase in the likelihood that a home would be burglarized. Also, the Brookings Institution reported that nearly half of a group of state prisoners said that they had stolen a gun at some point in their lives. In 14 percent of burglaries in which a gun was stolen, nothing else was taken. In some areas, police estimate that 50 percent of all handgun crimes are committed with stolen weapons. So, instead of protecting the homeowner, a gun may attract thieves and lead to future crimes.

In addition, the Uniform Crime Reports of the Federal Bureau of Investigation (FBI) show that out of 30,708 Americans who died by gunfire in 1998, only 316 were shot in self-defense by a private citizen. The following year, the FBI counted only 154 justifiable firearms homicides by private citizens, out of 8,259 firearms murders in the United States. A University of California study found that gun owners are nearly twice as likely to be killed by firearms as those who do not keep firearms at home.

Those who oppose gun control, on the other hand, say that self-defense statistics should count more than those incidents in which a burglar or mugger was killed. If the survey is changed to include criminals who were scared away by the possibility of fac-

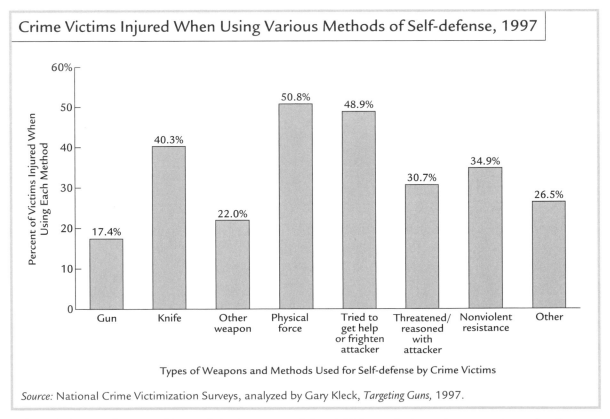

Crime Victims Injured When Using Various Methods of Self-defense, 1997

Source: National Crime Victimization Surveys, analyzed by Gary Kleck, *Targeting Guns,* 1997.

When victims are threatened by a criminal, some are injured. This graph shows the percentage of victims who were injured when they defended themselves in various ways.

ing an armed citizen, the self-defense statistics take an enormous jump. In 1997, criminologist Gary Kleck analyzed the National Crime Victimization Survey data collected by the U.S. Department of Justice. Kleck found that crime victims who resisted with a gun were less likely to suffer an injury or to be attacked by the criminal than those who used other methods of self-defense or those who did not resist the criminal at all.

According to another study by the Brookings Institution, 74 percent of a sampling of state prisoners said that they had avoided occupied houses for fear of being shot. A study for the Department of Justice found that 34 percent of criminals said that they had been "scared off, shot at, wounded, or captured by an armed victim." In the same study, 40 percent of criminals said that they had not committed crimes because they were afraid that the potential victim was armed. When Kennesaw, Georgia, passed a law requiring heads of households to have at least one firearm in the home, the burglary rate dropped 89 percent, compared to a decrease of 10.4 percent in the rest of the state. These findings support the idea that firearms provide effective defense for innocent homeowners.

Collectors

Some guns are never fired at all. Collectors who value their beauty or historical value acquire firearms for display or research. A collection may include weapons from a certain era—World War II, for example—or weapons of a particular type from many time periods.

ILLEGAL GUN USE

If only law-abiding citizens owned firearms, very few people would argue about gun control. However, firearms are frequently employed by the nation's criminals. A survey by the U.S. Department of Justice reported that in 2002, nearly 354,000 crime victims said that they had faced a criminal with a firearm. In recent years, the number of firearms-related crimes has fallen, as have firearms injuries.

The FBI found that in 2003, 42 percent of robberies and 19 percent of aggravated assaults (serious attacks) were committed with firearms. For murder, firearms are overwhelmingly the

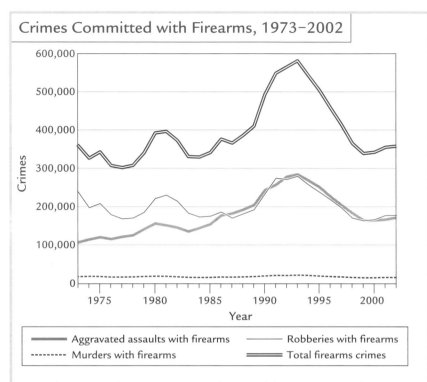

Crimes Committed with Firearms, 1973–2002

Legend:
— Aggravated assaults with firearms   — Robberies with firearms
---- Murders with firearms   === Total firearms crimes

Note: The Bureau of Justice Statistics, a division of the Department of Justice, surveys how many crimes were committed each year in the United States with firearms. Crimes include the UCR index offenses of murder, robbery, and aggravated assault.
Source: FBI, The Uniform Crime Reports (UCR).

MURDER WEAPONS, 2002

Region	Total[1] (all weapons)	Firearms	Knives or Cutting Instruments	Unknown or Other Dangerous Weapons	Personal Weapons[2] (hands, fists, feet, etc.)
Total	100.0	66.7	12.6	14.1	6.6
Northeast	100.0	62.6	17.4	12.6	7.5
Midwest	100.0	66.4	10.3	16.5	6.8
South	100.0	66.9	12.1	14.6	6.4
West	100.0	68.9	12.3	12.4	6.4

[1] Because of rounding, the percentages may not add to 100.0.
[2] Pushed is included in personal weapons.

Note: The Bureau of Justice Statistics, a division of the Department of Justice, surveys which weapons were used to commit murder. This chart shows the results for 2002.
Source: Bureau of Justice Statistics, Department of Justice.

HOW MURDERS ARE COMMITTED, 1998–2002

Weapons	1998	1999	2000	2001[1]	2002
Total	14,209	13,011	13,230	14,061	14,054
Total firearms:	9,220	8,480	8,661	8,890	9,369
Handguns	7,405	6,658	6,778	6,931	7,176
Rifles	546	400	411	386	480
Shotguns	626	531	485	511	476
Other guns	16	92	53	59	74
Firearms, type not stated	627	799	934	1,003	1,163
Knives or cutting instruments	1,890	1,712	1,782	1,831	1,767
Blunt objects (clubs, hammers, etc.)	750	756	617	680	666
Personal weapons[2] (hands, fists, feet, etc.)	959	885	927	961	933
Poison	6	11	8	12	23
Explosives	10	0	9	4	11
Fire	132	133	134	109	104
Narcotics	33	26	20	37	48
Drowning	28	28	15	23	18
Strangulation	213	190	166	153	143
Asphyxiation	99	106	92	116	103
Other weapons or weapons not stated	869	684	799	1,245	869

[1] The murder and nonnegligent homicides that occurred as a result of the events of September 11, 2001, are not included.
[2] Pushed is included in personal weapons.

Source: Bureau of Justice Statistics, Department of Justice.

weapon of choice. In 2003, 67 percent of all homicides were committed with a gun.

FBI statistics also show that when law officers are killed, firearms are nearly always responsible. For example, 51 of the 56 police officers who died on duty in 2002 were killed by firearms. Handguns were responsible for 38 of the fatal shootings.

Law officers are not the only victims of gunfire. Firearms are also involved in accidental shootings. A gun may go off while it is being cleaned, or a child may pull a trigger without understanding the consequences of this action. All these incidents add up. According

MURDER OF LAW ENFORCEMENT PERSONNEL, 1973–2000

Year	Total Killed	With Handguns	With Other Guns	Other Methods
1973	134	93	34	7
1974	132	95	33	4
1975	129	93	34	2
1976	111	66	28	17
1977	93	59	24	10
1978	93	67	24	2
1979	106	76	24	6
1980	104	69	26	9
1981	91	69	17	5
1982	92	60	22	10
1983	80	54	20	6
1984	72	46	20	6
1985	78	58	12	8
1986	66	51	11	4
1987	74	49	18	7
1988	78	63	13	2
1989	66	40	17	9
1990	66	48	9	9
1991	71	50	18	3
1992	64	44	11	9
1993	70	50	17	3
1994	79	66	12	1
1995	74	43	19	12
1996	61	50	7	4
1997	70	49	18	3
1998	61	40	18	3
1999	42	25	16	1
2000	51	33	14	4
2001	70	45	15	10
2002	56	38	13	5
2003	52	34	11	7

Note: When law enforcement personnel are murdered, the weapon is usually a firearm.
Source: FBI, Law Enforcement Officers Killed and Assaulted, 1973–2000.

to the Centers for Disease Control, a U.S. government agency, in 2000, 28,663 Americans died from firearms injury. (This number includes accidents and suicides as well as murders.)

Suicide

Suicide took the lives of 30,622 Americans in 2001, according to the Centers for Disease Control. Of those deaths, 55 percent, involved firearms, and 3,971 of the victims were young people between the ages of 15 and 24. The National Center for Health

---

PUBLIC OPINION AND GUN CONTROL

The National Opinion Research Center at the University of Chicago surveyed Americans' views on gun control in 1999. Though few people want guns outlawed completely, most Americans favor some sort of control, including these measures:

- 82 percent support a required police permit before purchase of a gun
- 81 percent want a background check and a waiting period before purchase of a gun
- 80 percent favor requiring registration of handguns, and 61 percent want long guns (rifles, shotguns) registered also
- 80 percent believe that only people 21 and older should be able to buy a handgun
- 79 percent support background checks for resales of guns between private individuals
- 70 percent agree that gun control laws should be stricter, "even if it means that it will be harder for law-abiding citizens to purchase handguns"

The Roper Center for Public Opinion Research found in 2003 that 78 percent of Americans disapproved of holding gunmakers responsible if judges or juries find that their products were used to commit a crime. A 1998 survey by Lawrence Research of registered voters resulted in these statistics:

- 85 percent of Americans believe that people have the right to defend themselves in their homes
- 64 percent say that law-abiding citizens should be allowed to carry firearms for protection outside their homes
- 72 percent want stricter sentences for convicted criminals who used guns in their crimes, rather than more gun laws

Statistics calculates that when young people commit suicide, more than half do so with a gun. At the other end of the age range, about 73 percent of suicides by elderly people were committed with firearms.

A large number of Americans "keep and bear arms" legally every day, for sport and self-defense. Those who oppose gun control laws tend to focus on this group when arguing their views, but statistics also show that another large segment of the population uses guns to kill, wound, or threaten others. Supporters of gun control refer to these crimes when making a case for strict regulations. Each side has amassed evidence and arguments to support its point of view.

7

The Case for Gun Control

One supporter of gun control has had a lot of time to think about the issue; he has also had some personal experience with firearms. John Hinckley, Jr., has been in a mental hospital for more than 20 years because he attempted to assassinate President Ronald Reagan. Hinckley purchased his weapon in Rocky's Pawn Shop in Dallas, Texas. He filled out the form required by law: No, he wrote, he was not a drug addict; no, he had never been convicted of a major

> "If somebody like me can buy six Saturday Night Specials, there is something drastically wrong."
>
> —*John Hinckley, Jr., gunman who attempted to assassinate President Ronald Reagan*

In 1981, moments before being hit by a bullet from John Hinckley's gun, President Ronald Reagan waved to the crowd outside a Washington, D.C., hotel. *(Ronald Reagan Library)*

crime; and no, he was not mentally ill. (This last statement was incorrect.) On March 30, 1981, he aimed his new handgun at Reagan and his press secretary, James Brady. Both were severely injured, as were two others in the crowd. From his hospital room, Hinckley has argued that stricter gun control laws would have prevented the shooting.

Supporters of strict gun control regulations agree with John Hinckley. They cite statistics such as the following to make their case:

- According to U.S. government statistics, since 1960, more than 1 million Americans have died in firearm-related murders, suicides, and accidents. This number does not include deaths in combat.
- A 1997 survey by the Centers for Disease Control of 26 countries found that 86 percent of the world total of firearms deaths of children under the age of 15 occurred in the United States.
- An international medical journal reported that in 1998 the number of Americans who died as a result of firearms was eight times greater than the total number of firearms deaths in 25 other countries combined.
- *The Journal of the American Medical Association* calculated the cost of providing medical care for firearms injuries in 1995 at approximately $4 billion.

Statistics tell only part of the story. To back up their arguments, gun control supporters also point to a string of horrifying shooting sprees, including some in schools. These crimes include

- **The Washington, D.C., sniper killings:** During three weeks in October 2002, residents of the nation's capital and the surrounding area were terrified by a series of random killings. Thirteen people were shot, and 10 died. John Muhammad and Lee Malvo have been convicted of these crimes.
- **Columbine High School:** In Littleton, Colorado, on April 20, 1999, two boys—Dylan Klebold and Eric Harris—opened fire on their classmates. They killed 13 and wounded 21 before turning their guns on themselves.
- **Thurston High School:** On May 21, 1998, 15-year-old Kip Kinkel killed two students and wounded 25 more in Spring-

"A gun is money with a trigger."

—*burglar, quoted in a report by the Brookings Institution about guns and self-defense*

field, Oregon. When authorities went to his home to investigate, they found that Kinkel had murdered his parents as well.

To those who favor gun control laws, each new shooting incident and every statistic is further proof that the government has to do more to stop firearms violence.

CRIME AND SELF-DEFENSE

It happens dozens of times a day. A homeowner returns to find a window smashed or a lock forced. The television is missing, drawers are overturned, and the jewelry box is empty. Or, even more horribly, a mugging, a rape, or a kidnapping occurs. In these situations, many people turn to firearms. If a criminal threatens again, they think, the gun will provide protection.

A gun in the home probably will not protect residents from a break-in. According to the FBI, nearly all burglaries occur when no one is at home. Furthermore, in the fear and confusion of a burglary, a homeowner may not be able to locate the weapon in time to use it effectively. If the handgun is found in time, pro–gun control groups point out that the weapon may not offer much protection. A criminal may gain control of the weapon during a struggle, even if the gun owner is a trained professional. According to the FBI, 7 percent of the law enforcement professionals killed by gunfire while on duty in 2002 were shot with their own weapon.

Another issue involves children and firearms. A loaded gun that is handy for the adults of the house is also accessible to children. In 2000, more than 3,000 Americans under the age of 19 died from firearms injuries, according to the National Vital Statistics Report. Of course, children may be harmed by many things other than guns. However, the same report found that approximately 25 percent of young people's firearms injuries resulted in death. Children seriously hurt in other ways died only once in 760 cases.

Adults, too, are at risk. According to the Department of Justice, about 57 percent of all murders involve family or friends. Many of these crimes take place without planning, in a moment of anger or jealousy. Clearly, violence and harm can come to adults from other

> "People who are shot are . . . more likely to die than people injured with non-gun weapons."
>
> —*Douglas J. Wiebe, author of a University of California at Los Angeles study on the relationship between gun ownership and firearms injury, 2003*

sources, too. But gun control supporters argue that firearms cause serious or fatal wounds more easily than some other weapons, such as fists or knives. Also, with firearms, murderers, muggers, and other criminals do not even have to touch their victims to cause harm. They pull the trigger, and the bullet goes out instantly—an effortless act.

ASSASSINATIONS

Hinckley's shot at President Reagan was just one of a long list of attempts or successful firearms assassinations of American leaders.

ASSASSINATIONS AND ATTEMPTED ASSASSINATIONS OF U.S. LEADERS

Victim	Year	Result
Andrew Jackson	1835	attempt
Abraham Lincoln	1865	killed
James Garfield	1881	killed
William McKinley	1901	killed
Theodore Roosevelt (ex-president)	1912	wounded
Franklin Roosevelt	1933	attempt
Harry Truman	1950	attempt
John F. Kennedy	1963	killed
Robert Kennedy (presidential candidate)	1968	killed
George Wallace (presidential candidate)	1972	wounded
Gerald Ford	1975	two attempts
Ronald Reagan	1981	wounded

If the list is expanded to include more than government leaders, many others, such as musicians John Lennon and Jam Master Jay of Run DMC and civil rights crusader Martin Luther King, Jr., could be added.

Gun control supporters believe that the availability of firearms is an important factor in the large number of assassinations in the United States. Given that the president and most other celebrities appear in public only when they are surrounded by bodyguards, criminals armed with knives or other non-firearm weapons are not likely to get close enough to do damage. Guns, however, can do harm even from a distance.

SUICIDE

The journal *Injury Prevention* studied the relationship between suicide rates and firearms. An article published in 2002 showed that the number of handguns in circulation is related to the number of suicides. The more American households with handguns, the higher the suicide rate. Similarly, a 2002 University of California study reported that people with guns at home are 16 times more likely to commit suicide using firearms.

Opponents of gun control laws say that if people want to commit suicide, they will do so no matter what. If a gun is not available, they point out, many other weapons are. However, people who recover from suicide attempts may receive treatment and go on to live normal lives. The key word here is *recover*. Since most handguns can kill instantly, bullets allow few second chances.

President Franklin Delano Roosevelt was once the target of an assassination attempt. *(National Archives)*

WHY SUPPORTERS WANT FEDERAL LAWS

New York City has one of the strictest gun control laws in the nation. Citizens applying for a permit to carry a concealed handgun must show that they need such protection, and a large number of applications are denied. Yet, in spite of its tough laws, the New York City Police Department estimates that as many as 2 million illegal guns were in circulation in the city in a recent year.

New York's gun laws have not made the city a safer place. The reason, according to gun control supporters, is simple. Most of the guns seized by the police in New York City were not bought there. In fact, the Bureau of Alcohol, Tobacco, Firearms, and Explosives announced that in 1999, 80 percent of the guns used to commit crimes in New York City could be traced to a handful of southern states, all of which have much less strict gun laws.

"Where there are more guns, there are more suicides."

—*David Hemenway, Harvard University School of Public Health, 2002*

> "Criminals and terrorists know they can get guns, no questions asked, at gun shows in many states. To protect New York children, we need federal legislation."
>
> —*Edie Smith, Million Mom March, New York City chapter, 2002*

To gun control supporters, the solution is simple. The federal government should pass stricter laws, which would apply to every state in the Union. In a patchwork, state-by-state system, no place can protect itself from guns bought elsewhere, especially from handguns, which are small and easily hidden.

To show the effectiveness of gun control laws, activists sometimes compare the number of firearms murders in the United States with statistics from foreign countries. Where guns laws are strict, the murder rate tends to be extremely low.

ADDITIONAL LAWS ARE NEEDED

Pro–gun control groups want a federal law requiring all handgun owners to be licensed, just as drivers of automobiles are licensed.

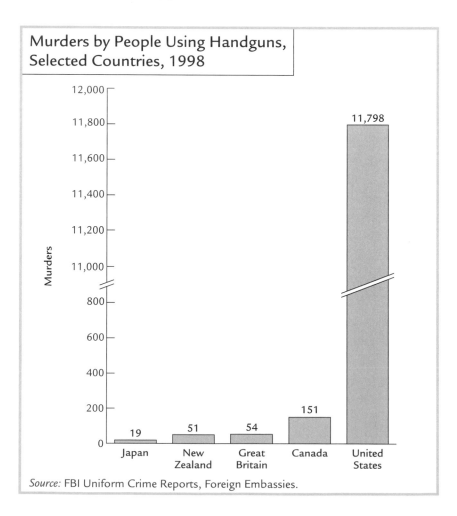

Murders by People Using Handguns, Selected Countries, 1998

Source: FBI Uniform Crime Reports, Foreign Embassies.

WHEN STRICT GUN CONTROLS ARE IN EFFECT
The Path to a Permit

Anyone who applies for a gun permit in New York City must follow a lengthy procedure, mandated by the city's strict laws. In 2004, this was the procedure:

- Applicants fill out a four-page form explaining their reasons for wanting a gun and detailing the last five places they worked, any arrests and/or convictions, medicines they take, psychological problems, any rejections from civil service jobs, and times when they have testified in court. Applicants must also explain how they will safeguard their weapons.
- Applicants must promise that they know the city gun laws, are willing to take gun safety training courses, and have not used illegal drugs.
- Applicants have their fingerprints taken and pay $354 in fees.
- The New York City Police Department checks the information on the application.
- Applicants are interviewed in person at police headquarters. They may be asked to provide more information, such as tax records.

If successful, applicants may purchase a gun, which must be taken to police headquarters for inspection. The whole process takes about six weeks.

***

Before a license is issued, the applicant would take a safety course, have fingerprints taken, and provide proof of address. These last two measures are intended to stop criminals from using false IDs. The license would have to be renewed every few years, just as drivers' licenses are. Upon renewal, law enforcement officials could check to see that the license holder had not committed any crimes and to deny licenses to anyone not eligible to possess a handgun.

Gun control supporters also want guns, especially handguns, to be registered with local or state police. If the government is capable of keeping track of cars, say pro–gun control groups, it can and should keep track of firearms as well. With a national registration system, guns used to commit a crime could be traced quickly.

Many states now track the first sale of a gun but not the resale. According to gun control supporters, many criminals purchase weapons at gun shows or over the Internet, where some types of sales do not have to be reported. Nationwide handgun registration would close the gun show and Internet loopholes and allow all firearms to be tracked.

The Brady Campaign to Prevent Gun Violence, as well as many other pro–gun control organizations, also wants Congress to put a true waiting period back into the Brady Bill. The Brady Bill, which took effect in 1994, originally required gun purchasers to wait five days between buying and taking possession of a firearm. During the waiting period, a thorough background check could be made to ensure that the purchaser was not forbidden by law to possess a firearm. That waiting period was phased out in 1998, when a national computerized checking system was created. Some important records, however, are not included in the checking system— for example, many states do not computerize mental health records—so the computer system may allow an ineligible person to purchase a gun. A five-day waiting period will allow for more thorough checking. Also, if the gun purchaser was upset and planning a crime, the waiting period might allow the purchaser to calm down, thus preventing violence.

GUN CONTROL AND THE SECOND AMENDMENT

Will these measures limit Americans' Second Amendment rights? No, say gun control supporters. The "right to keep and bear arms" has never been unlimited, they point out, either in the United States or in England, the origin of the American legal tradition. The founders, argue pro–gun controllers, intended to protect the rights of the states, not to ensure that individual Americans had access to firearms. Supporters of gun control regulations also cite the many Supreme Court rulings favoring the militia view, which interprets the right to bear arms as applying to state militias. Court cases opposing the militia view come from lower courts, though the wording of some Supreme Court opinions does sometimes lend support to both sides of the debate.

Gun control supporters also point out that strict rules for licensing, registration, and use have not affected Americans' ability to drive and own cars. Automobile laws are seldom questioned—how much more important, they say, to regulate weapons. Gun control laws help to protect law-abiding citizens from gun violence by criminals and do not disarm the general public.

PRO-GUN CONTROL GROUPS

A number of Americans are working very hard to tighten the nation's gun control laws. One of the most famous is the Brady Campaign to Prevent Gun Violence, which was originally called Handgun Control, Inc. It was renamed after James and Sarah Brady in 2001. James Brady, press secretary to President Ronald Reagan, was wounded in an assassination attempt in 1981. His wife, Sarah, became chair of the Center to Prevent Handgun Violence in 1991. The Brady Campaign to Prevent Gun Violence lobbies Congress for tighter gun laws. It maintains a Web site with articles on many gun-related issues, including proposed laws and statistics about gun violence. The Brady Campaign also provides information on petitions and demonstrations for citizens who want to work for stricter gun control.

PRO-GUN CONTROL ACTIVISTS IN CONGRESS

Until December 7, 1993, Carolyn McCarthy was a nurse living quietly in a suburb of New York City with her husband and son. On December 7, a mentally ill man boarded the 5:33 P.M. commuter train leaving the city. About a half hour later, he pulled out a Ruger P-89 9mm pistol and began to fire in the train car. After reloading three times, he was wrestled to the ground by several passengers. Six people were killed, including McCarthy's husband, and 19 more were wounded, one of them her son. McCarthy began a campaign against gun violence that led her to run for the House of Representatives, where she has now served four terms.

Senator Ted Kennedy is also no stranger to violence. His brothers, John and Robert, were both assassinated with firearms. President John Kennedy was hit by a sniper shot in 1963, and Robert was killed with a handgun in 1968, while he was running for president. Ted Kennedy and Carolyn McCarthy are two of the strongest supporters of tight gun control laws in the federal government.

The Brady Campaign works with the Million Mom March. The original Million Mom March was a demonstration in Washington, D.C., on Mother's Day in 2000. About 750,000 people demonstrated on the National Mall, and many more marched in towns and cities across the country. The "Million Moms" called on lawmakers to pass stricter gun control laws. Presently, the Million Mom March sponsors many local groups of gun control supporters and provides help for victims and survivors of firearms violence.

The Violence Policy Center (VPC) also works to promote firearms regulation. The VPC views gun violence as a health crisis. The VPC researches gun policy, educates the public about its findings, and lobbies for change. Each year, the VPC issues 15–20 reports on gun-related issues, including guns and product safety lawsuits, domestic violence and firearms, and the youth gun culture.

8

The Case Against Gun Control

The Second Amendment grants the right that "makes all the other rights possible." Such is the view of people who oppose gun control regulations. They add that because a large number of Americans exercise their Second Amendment right to own firearms, the government cannot become all powerful. An armed citizenry, they believe, will not let anyone limit the traditional freedoms of American citizens, particularly the rights granted in the U.S. Constitution and the Bill of Rights.

In the same line of reasoning, gun control opponents believe that laws curbing the right of Americans to own or use firearms are unconstitutional, dangerous, and useless. They firmly support the idea that the Second Amendment created an individual right to "keep and bear arms." Further, they say that gun control laws hurt society because, as anti–gun controllers put it, "If guns are outlawed, only outlaws will have guns." In addition, they maintain that the thousands of gun control laws on the books have not been effective in stopping violent crime.

> "To preserve liberty, it is essential that the whole body of people always possess arms and be taught alike, especially when young, how to use them."
>
> —*Richard Henry Lee*, Letters from the Federal Farmer to the Republican, *1787*

THE SECOND AMENDMENT AND THE CONSTITUTION

The Second Amendment clearly states that the "right of the people to keep and bear arms" should not be violated. The definition of *people* is key to understanding the meaning of the amendment. Those who favor gun control laws stand firmly behind the idea that *the people* in the Second Amendment refers to state governments, which have the right to form militias. Those who oppose

85

In *Letters from the Federal Farmer to the Republican,* Richard Henry Lee (1732–94) urged young people to learn to use firearms "to preserve liberty." *(National Archives)*

gun control, however, interpret *the people* to refer literally to the people of the United States. Thus they believe that the Second Amendment is a right held by individual Americans.

One Supreme Court case, *United States v. Verdugo-Urquidez* (1990), defined *the people* in a way that favors the individual rights view. The Court wrote that the phrase *the people* in the Second Amendment, as well as in other amendments, refers to "a class of persons who are part of a national community or who have . . . sufficient [enough] connection with this country to be considered part of that community."

Another famous Supreme Court case also supported the individual rights view. In *Dred Scott v. Sandford,* a case concerning freed slaves that was tried in 1857, the Court ruled that black Americans were not citizens. If they were citizens, said the Court, they would have the right "to keep and carry arms wherever they went."

Anti–gun controllers also point out a well-established principle of American law: People may be punished when they break the law, but they are not usually restrained or limited ahead of time just because someday they might break the law. One gun rights group compares the effect of gun control laws to limits on the right to freedom of speech, guaranteed by the First Amendment. Americans generally enjoy the right to say whatever they like. However, it is against the law to shout, "Fire!" in a crowded movie theater when no danger threatens because the resulting panic may injure someone. No one suggests that moviegoers should be gagged when they buy a ticket as a preventive measure against someone's breaking the law during the show. In the same way, say anti–gun controllers, no one without a criminal record should be prevented from buying firearms for fear that someday the buyer may misuse the weapon. Authorities should wait until a crime is committed rather than risk disarming innocent citizens.

People who oppose gun control also object to licensing and registration. Owning a gun is not, they say, the same as owning or driving a car, a comparison often made by people on the other side of the debate. Automobile use on public highways is a privilege.

Gun ownership is a right guaranteed by the U.S. Constitution, anti–gun controllers maintain.

A GRADUAL LOSS OF RIGHTS

Most pro-gun people accept some limitations on the right to keep and bear arms—laws forbidding weapons to children, violent criminals, and the mentally ill, for example. Many of the same people worry, however, that current gun control laws are like the thin end of a wedge that will pry open the door to a widespread ban on firearms.

To support this opinion, anti–gun controllers point to several countries, including Canada, where a 1934 law required registration of handguns. After 1977, Canadians needed a certificate to purchase a firearm. Buyers had to show that they needed the weapon, and protection of property was not accepted as a reason to own a gun. In 1995, Canada banned certain types of handguns completely. By 2003, all rifles and shotguns had to be registered. Furthermore, Canadian police are allowed to enter homes without search warrants to check for unregistered guns.

Another argument advanced by people opposed to gun control concerns the rights of minorities. As the *Dred Scott* case shows, at various times in American history, the majority power has attempted to keep guns out of the hands of minorities. In the colonial era, for example, British authorities did not want Native Americans to own firearms. Anti–gun controllers believe that weapons laws may easily become a tool to disarm and therefore to control anyone whose race, religion, or ethnic background is seen as a threat by the majority.

CRIME AND SELF-DEFENSE

Guns do not kill; people do. This statement reflects the view of people who oppose gun control laws. In their eyes, blaming the weapon for the crime is illogical and wrong. Pro–gun controllers sometimes praise Great Britain's strict gun laws, crediting these regulations for the fact that murder by handgun is extremely rare in that country. However, Great Britain also has much lower rates of homicide by hands, feet, and knives than in the United States. Anti–gun controllers point out that no one has ever suggested that

"The right of self-defense . . . is founded in the law of nature, and is not, nor can be, superseded [replaced] by any law of society."

—*Sir Michael Foster, judge of the king's court, late 18th century*

"A Warning should be sounded to legislators against passing laws which on the face of them seem to make it impossible for a criminal to get a pistol, if the same laws would make it very difficult for an honest man and a good citizen to obtain them."

—*James Drain, president of the National Rifle Association, circa 1907*

American hands and feet are to blame for the higher rate of murder with these "weapons." Certainly no one thinks that a ban on hands and feet, or knives, is a good idea. Firearms, say gun control opponents, should not be singled out by special laws.

Much more important in the control of crime, say anti–gun control groups, is pressure from society to respect laws and to obey proper authorities. If criminals are promptly and severely punished, the theory goes, crime will drop regardless of the number of guns in circulation. Thus they strongly support stiff prison sentences for crimes committed with firearms.

People on both sides of the debate acknowledge that the police are the best defense against crime and violence; however, opponents of gun control point out that the police are often understaffed and are hard pressed to protect everyone. In 2003, an average of 150,000 police officers were on duty at any given time to protect a population of more than 250 million Americans, according to the American Firearms Association. The Department of Justice found that in a recent year, police officers failed to respond within one hour to 168,881 crimes of violence. Also, in *Warren v. District of Columbia* (1981), the U.S. Court of Appeals for the District of Columbia Circuit ruled that the government has a general duty to provide protection for citizens but no obligation to protect any particular citizen. The court added that there is "no constitutional right to be protected by the state against being murdered by criminals or madmen." All these facts add up to one conclusion, say anti–gun controllers: Citizens must be allowed to protect themselves.

Opponents of gun control also state that most guns are never involved in crime, and neither are most gun owners. States issuing gun permits often require that these permits be canceled if the owner has committed a serious crime. Only a tiny percentage of these permits have had to be taken away by states. In Florida, for instance, just 0.02 percent of firearms permits were canceled between October 1987 and February 2002. In Wyoming, only 0.3 percent of permits were taken away between October 1994 and February 2002. Many other states post similar numbers.

Those who oppose gun control also point to the fact that some societies with very high rates of gun ownership and usage have extremely low rates of firearms crime. In Switzerland, for example, every law-abiding male Swiss citizen of military age is issued a firearm, which is kept at home, even when active military service is over. Yet violent gun crimes are extremely rare in Switzerland. In 2000, for example, Swiss police reported only 40 murders with firearms. In the United States, the number of guns in circulation increases every year, yet the nation's violent crime rate has decreased every year for more than two decades, according to FBI statistics.

SUICIDE AND ACCIDENTS

One argument often stated by gun control supporters is that easily available guns contribute to high suicide rates, but opponents of gun control feel that this link has not been proved. A 2000 study in the *Journal of the American Medical Association* examined suicide rates for adults aged 22–55 after passage of the Brady Bill, which established a required five-day waiting period between the purchase and possession of a handgun. Supporters of a required waiting period believe that a few days may act as a "cooling-off period" for seriously depressed people, during which some would-be suicides may change their minds. Yet the study found no significant drop in suicides after the waiting period was put in place except among adults over the age of 55. The suicide rate for that particular group did fall, but the rates for other age groups remained nearly the same.

Gun control opponents also point to Japan to disprove the link between suicide and the availability of firearms. Japan's gun laws are extremely strict. Rifles and handguns are prohibited, and shotguns are subject to many regulations. Yet in recent years about 90 Japanese a day have committed suicide, mostly without firearms, according to the *New York Times*. These statistics, say anti–gun controllers, show that suicide is a matter of culture and individual choice, not a result of gun availability.

The cause of suicide, argue anti–gun controllers, is not the weapon but the mental condition of the people who kill themselves. The *Journal of Clinical Psychiatry* found that more than 90 percent of the children and teenagers who committed suicide were suffering from a mental disorder. Stress and poor relationships with parents are also risk factors for child and teen suicide. Prohibiting firearms, they state, will not change the mental health of potential suicide victims.

GUN SAFETY FOR YOUNG PEOPLE

Since 1988, more than 17 million schoolchildren have participated in the Eddie Eagle GunSafe Program, sponsored by the National Rifle Association. Children learn that if they see an "unattended" gun, one that is not being taken care of by an adult, they should do four things:

- ◆ Stop
- ◆ Do not touch

- ◆ Leave the area
- ◆ Tell an adult

The goal of the Eddie Eagle program is to decrease the number of accidental firearms injuries among young children.

Similarly, anti–gun controllers point out that more injuries occur annually from car crashes than from gun-related incidents, according to the National Center for Injury Prevention and Control (NCIPC), but no one blames the automobile and calls for a ban on cars. The NCIPC also reports that since 1962, the death rate from gun accidents has been low and generally decreasing. True safety, say anti–gun controllers, comes from education and personal responsibility. Rather than blame the weapon, they prefer to see young people enrolled in firearms safety classes, such as the Eddie Eagle GunSafe Program taught by the National Rifle Association.

THE EFFECTIVENESS OF GUN CONTROL LAWS

People who oppose gun control laws believe that the evidence is clear: Gun control laws, they say, do not work. About 20,000 laws regulating firearms are already on the books, yet America is not free of gun violence. No new laws are needed, say anti–gun controllers, because more laws will be just as ineffective as the ones that now exist. The problem, they say, is that criminals by definition do not obey laws. In addition, the laws already on the books are not always enforced. A 2003 study by researchers at the University of California at Los Angeles found that half of firearms dealers questioned in an undercover survey were willing to allow buyers to purchase guns in violation of federal law.

Anti–gun controllers also point out that some of the new laws favored by gun control groups are not realistic. A "smart" gun that could be fired only by its owner is a great idea, they say; however, the technology to create such a gun does not exist. So when New Jersey recently passed a law requiring manufacturers to ensure that their handguns are "smart," the state imposed an unreasonable requirement. The real purpose of the law, say anti–gun controllers, is to move toward a complete ban on handguns.

The real way to decrease gun violence, in the opinion of those opposing gun control, is to enforce the laws against violent crime and to crack down on criminals who possess firearms. That is what the city of Richmond, Virginia, did in 1997 when it began a program called Project Exile. The state and local law enforcement officers went after firearms owned by felons (people who had been convicted of a serious crime). In one year, the number of murders dropped 41 percent from their high point in 1994, and crimes committed with firearms decreased 65 percent.

GROUPS OPPOSING GUN CONTROL

The best-known anti–gun control group is the National Rifle Association (NRA), which is headquartered in Washington, D.C. Retired army officers established the NRA in 1871 to improve the marksmanship of members. The founding officers were discouraged by the poor gun skills of the troops who had fought in the Civil War. The NRA still works to improve gun skills; one of its goals is to "train members of law enforcement agencies, the armed forces, the militia, and people of good repute [reputation] in marksmanship and in the safe handling and efficient use of small arms." The NRA holds classes for police officers and security guards in firearms safety and use. The NRA also sponsors pistol competitions for law enforcement officers and others. In 1975, the NRA formed the Institute for Legislative Action, or ILA. The ILA analyzes proposed laws and lobbies for the individual rights view of the Second Amendment.

CHARLTON HESTON
Actor and Activist

Charlton Heston, during a long film career that began after World War II, played a wide range of roles, including Moses, Michelangelo, a circus performer, and a cowboy. Perhaps his most satisfying role took place offstage: Heston was president of the National Rifle Association from 1998 to 2003. A longtime supporter of an individual's right to keep and bear arms, Heston is famous for holding a gun high in the air and declaring that he would let the weapon be taken only from his "cold, dead hand."

Charlton Heston, then president of the National Rifle Association, addressed the group in 2000. *(Robert Padgett/Reuters/Landov)*

The Second Amendment Foundation shares the belief of the Citizens' Committee for the Right to Keep and Bear Arms that "the disarming of individual law-abiding citizens will result in the loss of individual freedoms." Both organizations work to educate the public about the individual rights interpretation of the Second Amendment. The Citizens' Committee also lobbies for this view in Congress, as does Gun Owners of America.

The National Shooting Sports Foundation aims to achieve "a better understanding and a more active participation in the shooting sports," including hunting and target shooting. It was created in 1961 by manufacturers and sellers of firearms, ammunition, and other gun-related products and other firearms-related businesses.

9

The Second and Third Amendments Today and in the Future

At every airport, lines of travelers slowly snake through security checks. They walk through metal detectors and allow their luggage—and sometimes their shoes—to be screened, searched, even swabbed for traces of explosives. Most Americans submit to these strict security measures without protest, but just a few years ago, these procedures would have produced many howls of outrage. The different reactions may be explained by one historic date: September 11, 2001. The terrorist attacks on the World Trade Center and the Pentagon destroyed buildings and lives, but they also created a new world. In the 21st century, all Americans are aware

This mural of names honors those who died in the terrorist attack on the World Trade Center in New York City. *(Peter Foley/EPA/Landov)*

The National Guard has always helped out in times of emergency, as shown above protecting a storm damaged home in 1955. Since September 11, 2001, one is more likely to see armed National Guards protecting train stations or airports. *(National Archives, Department of Agriculture)*

of violence, and most have adjusted their daily habits at least slightly.

In this new reality, a number of Americans have come to believe that exchanging traditional liberties for additional safety is a good bargain. Others feel that it is more important than ever to preserve the American heritage of freedom and civil rights. These two reactions to terrorist threats have colored the debate about the Second Amendment. Discussion of the ban on assault rifles, for example, now includes references to terrorists as well as to neighborhood gangs. Even the Third Amendment may come under new consideration. If danger threatens Americans, will the government ever feel the need to quarter troops in private buildings? If so, will Americans open their homes willingly?

"The Second Amendment is the original Homeland Security Act!"

—*Florida governor Jeb Bush, April 2003, speaking about U.S. law to combat terrorism*

September 11th also underlined how truly interconnected the countries of the world are. The gun laws of one nation may express perfectly its citizens' views on the proper role of firearms. But as people move freely and frequently across borders, so do their ideas and habits. It is no longer enough to know the gun laws of one's home country. An international perspective is important also. All these factors add up to one statement: The debate about the Second Amendment and all American rights is more complicated now than ever before.

GUNS AND TERRORISM

In 2002, U.S. forces invading a terrorist camp in Kabul, Afghanistan, found a frightening training manual. One section of the booklet was devoted to firearms. The manual explains to terrorists that guns are easily available in the United States. It goes on to tell members of al-Qaeda, the terrorist group responsible for the September 11, 2001, attacks, that they should "obtain an assault weapon legally, preferably AK-47 or variations," if they are living in the United States.

This manual is often mentioned by gun control activists as a reason to pass stricter laws regulating firearms. So is the fact that some terrorists have been caught purchasing firearms on U.S. soil. In 1999, for example, four members of the Irish Republican Army (IRA) spent more than $18,000 on handguns, rifles, and ammunition while in the United States. The IRA has claimed responsibility for violent acts in Northern Ireland and Great Britain. The weapons were purchased from a licensed U.S. dealer who agreed not to report the sales in exchange for extra money. The IRA men were caught when they tried to send the firearms overseas.

"We have a responsibility to deny weapons to terrorists and to actively prevent private citizens from providing them."

—*President George W. Bush, November 2001, speaking to the United Nations*

Gun control opponents respond with this fact: The hijackers who took control of four planes on September 11th were armed only with box cutters (a small cutting tool), not with guns. No one on the planes was able to fight back with firearms against the hijackers because passengers are screened for such weapons. Americans cannot resist terrorism, gun control opponents declare, by disarming its own people. Opponents of gun laws also point out that the terrorism/gun link is often a corrupt dealer who decides not to obey the laws already in place, as in the IRA case described above.

Firearms Regulations and Terrorism

The arguments over terrorism and guns follow the same line of reasoning already in place before 2001, although some new situations have become part of the debate. One concerns the Federal Firearms Transaction Record, a document that dealers must complete for each gun sale. By law these documents remain with the dealer, and no information is given to the government. Gun control supporters would like to see this information given to the Bureau of Alcohol, Tobacco, Firearms, and Explosives (ATF; *Explosives* was added to the bureau's name in 2003) to help reveal suspicious purchasing patterns. Currently, only sales of more than one handgun from a single dealer within five business days are reported. If all sales were reported, buyers of large quantities of weapons, including both handguns and rifles, could be checked for terrorist ties. Those who support gun rights believe that this proposal would result in nothing but a blizzard of paperwork, without hampering terrorists.

Another issue is the background checks required by the Brady Bill. The FBI has a new system that alerts counterterrorism agents when a suspected terrorist tries to buy guns. Justice Department regulations, however, do not permit information about gun buyers obtained during these checks to be turned over to authorities unless the purchase is prohibited (because the would-be buyer is mentally ill, too young, or convicted of a major crime, for example), as reported in November 2003 by the *Washington Post.* Therefore, if the sale goes through, regardless of who the buyer is, his or her address may not be revealed. One Justice Department official explained that suspicion of a crime, even terrorism, is not enough to take away a suspect's Second Amendment rights. The Justice Department does, however, allow the FBI three days to find an appropriate reason to deny the gun sale. If the FBI discovers something amiss—a buyer who is too young or not a legal resident, for example—the sale is denied and all information may be shared with counterterrorism agents.

Furthermore, the background check records must be destroyed if the sale was permitted. In 2003, the records were kept for 90 days—even after the purchaser had taken possession of the firearms—to allow for additional investigation, but a law proposed by the House of Representatives in 2004 would require the destruction of background check records one day after the sale is completed. Critics of

> "Being a suspected member of a terrorist organization doesn't disqualify a person from owning a gun any more than being under investigation for a non-terrorism felony [serious crime] would."
>
> —*unnamed Justice Department official, speaking to the* Washington Post *in November 2003*

> "We could have a nationwide lookout for a known terrorist within our borders, but if he obtained a weapon, the Justice Department's policy is to refuse to reveal his location to law enforcement officials."
>
> —*Senator Frank Lautenberg, speaking to the* Washington Post *in November 2003*

IMPROVING BACKGROUND CHECKS

"A criminal background check is only as good as the records provided by the system," said Representative Carolyn McCarthy of New York as she proposed a law that she dubbed "Our Lady of Peace Act." The name refers to a church where a mentally ill man shot to death a priest and a churchgoer as they attended mass in March 2002. McCarthy argues that the background checks required by the Brady Bill fail to screen out many people who are ineligible to buy a firearm, including the shooter at Our Lady of Peace. The man's mental records were not checked when he bought his rifle. The proposed legislation would require states to provide more information to the FBI about any individual who may not legally purchase a gun, including those who have been convicted of a crime, abused drugs, been dishonorably discharged from the military, or been committed to a mental hospital. McCarthy also cosponsored bills to require background checks at all gun shows where at least 75 guns are for sale. None of the bills has yet passed.

Representative Carolyn McCarthy of New York fights for stronger gun control laws. *(Courtesy of Representative McCarthy)*

the House bill believe that terrorists and other criminals who might have used a false name to slip through the background check cannot be caught in that time period. Supporters of the bill believe that legal gun purchasers have the right to privacy and should not come under investigation when they have done nothing wrong. The 24-hour period is long enough, they say, to screen out the guilty.

The same proposed law would also bar the ATF from requiring gun dealers to count their weapons once a year. The inventory is intended to catch "missing" firearms—those that are not in the store but not on record as being sold. A 2000 ATF report stated that "errors in inventory records [at federal firearms dealers] are a serious problem because a firearm missing from inventory cannot be traced." Without the ability to trace a weapon involved in a crime or a terrorist act, say gun control supporters, law enforcement officers are at a disadvantage. Gun rights supporters believe that requiring inventories will not stop corrupt dealers and will unfairly burden law-abiding business owners.

Also, those who favor gun control would like to see private individuals limited to one firearm purchase per month. Terrorists in the past have bought large quantities of weapons in a short period of time. In June 2001, a member of an Islamic extremist group from the nation of Trinidad and Tobago was arrested as he tried to purchase 60 assault rifles and 10 machine guns. He had previously told undercover agents that he intended to use the weapons to overthrow the government of his country. Ten years earlier, the same extremist group had set off a car bomb and attacked the legislature of Trinidad and Tobago with firearms. Many of their weapons in that incident—105 out of 135—had been purchased at gun shops and gun shows in Florida by one man. Gun control opponents counter with the argument that the vast majority of legally bought weapons are not involved in terrorism or in any sort of crime. To limit legal purchases, they say, restricts the Second Amendment rights of Americans without any real impact on terrorist violence.

The Debate over .50-Caliber Rifles and Other Weapons

A .50-caliber rifle is a powerful weapon. It can hit a target 1,500 meters (approximately 4,900 feet, or almost one mile) away, about five times as far as the range of an ordinary semiautomatic weapon. These firearms are marketed to hunters and target shooters, who use them legally and peacefully. However, with special ammunition, a bullet from a .50-caliber rifle can penetrate several inches of steel. Such a weapon could therefore be used to bring down a small, low-flying plane or to blow up a fuel tank.

At present, .50-caliber rifles may be sold by licensed dealers or at gun shows. In early 2002, the U.S. State Department barred the export of .50-caliber rifles for nonmilitary purposes. The debate about the future of this weapon rages. Some would like to ban these powerful guns to decrease the possibility of a .50-caliber rifle falling into the hands of terrorists. Others believe that the .50-caliber rifle itself is not a problem; according to a congressional report, very few of these weapons have ever been involved in a crime. The criminals or terrorists who might misuse these weapons should be the true focus of law enforcement efforts, according to supporters of gun rights.

The same arguments apply to assault weapons, powerful semiautomatic rifles. In 1994, Congress banned many types of assault

FIREARMS FINGERPRINTS AND SMART GUNS

The House of Representatives and the Senate are currently considering laws that "fingerprint" all new firearms before they are sold. If the law is passed, every new gun would be fired once and a record would be kept of the pattern made by the bullet. (Like human fingerprints, the pattern from each gun is unique.) The weapon can then be tracked more easily if it is used in a crime and the bullet is recovered. However, critics of the law charge that as a gun ages, the pattern changes, so the original "fingerprint" may not match the one found after a crime. Another proposal would require guns to have a mechanism that prevents the operation of the firearm by strangers. The "smart" gun would recognize approved users and remain locked to everyone else. Those who oppose this law say that smart-gun technology has not yet been invented.

weapons for a period of 10 years; nevertheless, gun companies have continued to manufacture and sell assault weapons, even after 1994, staying within the law by changing some characteristics of the weapons. As the law expired, discussion continued. President George W. Bush said that he supported extending the ban when it expired in 2004, but Congress took no action to renew the ban. Gun control groups, meanwhile, are pressing for an even stricter regulation that would also outlaw the slightly changed weapons. Gun rights supporters, on the other hand, favor doing away with the ban entirely. An assault weapon, they say, is not officially a type of gun but simply a rifle that looks more "military" than other weapons.

THE POLITICS OF GUN CONTROL

Pro– and anti–gun control groups do not divide perfectly along political party lines. Those who favor stricter gun control laws tend to be Democrats, while those who uphold an individual right to keep and bear arms are more likely to be Republicans. As is the case on any issue, however, each party has some who differ with the majority position. In addition, Americans' views on a given issue can be quite complex: Instead of being in favor of all regulations or of none, many people see merit in some laws, in certain situations, for particular groups.

Because the two major political parties generally come down on opposite sides of the gun control issue, a change of administration in Washington from Democrat to Republican or vice versa affects gun control enforcement. During the Democratic administration of Bill Clinton, for example, the background check records required by the Brady Bill were kept for six months. The six-month period allowed law officers to check for mistakes and to take back licenses that had been issued in error. When the Republican administration of George W. Bush came into power, Attorney General John Ashcroft ruled that the records be destroyed after 24 hours. (Because the Brady Bill did not specify a particular period of time, the Justice Department was free to decide how long the records were kept.) Regardless of political party, however, every administration must either change or obey the laws.

In 2004, Attorney General John Ashcroft announced that terrorists may be planning additional attacks on the United States. The issue of terrorism has led many people on both sides of the gun control debate to rethink their positions. *(Matthew Cavanaugh/EPA/Landov)*

Private citizens also have an effect on gun control issues. Working in organized groups or as individuals, Americans may lobby, or attempt to influence lawmakers, about their cause. Two of the most important lobbying groups, the National Rifle Association (NRA) and the Brady Campaign to Prevent Gun Violence, meet with public officials to argue their views. They also throw their support behind candidates for office, on the national, state, and local level.

Each side of the gun control debate has passionate supporters, both in Congress and among ordinary American citizens. Some opinion polls show that while the public is split on Second Amendment issues, people who oppose gun control are more likely to see that issue as a deciding factor when they go to the polls. Governor Jeb Bush of Florida, a gun rights supporter, addressed the NRA in May 2003 and informed members that in 2002, 21 of the 24 candidates for the U.S. Senate favored by the NRA were elected, representing a remarkable display of political influence. On the other hand, Representative Carolyn McCarthy was elected to Congress on the basis of her support for stricter gun control laws. Representative McCarthy's husband and son were shot by a mentally ill man in December 1993.

THE ROLE OF GUN MANUFACTURERS

If a dangerous toy injures the child who plays with it, the manufacturer may be sued. If the manufacturer is judged to be at fault, the child or the family may receive damages, money to pay for medical bills and to make up for the child's suffering. If an improperly made gun misfires, however, the user may not sue the manufacturer. Guns are not covered by this type of law, which is known as "product liability."

Nevertheless, since 1989 gun manufacturers have found themselves in court again and again, defending their business practices. Several cities have sued, claiming that gun manufacturers are not careful enough when they distribute their products. By selling large quantities of weapons to shady dealers, critics claim, the manufacturers are allowing their products to fall into the hands of criminals. When the guns cause injuries or deaths, the lawsuits charge, the manufacturers should pay the bill.

"Those who manufacture and sell guns in this country owe a duty to use reasonable care, to do what they can to prevent people like this crazed shooter [a gunman who opened fire on preschoolers in California in 1999] from obtaining guns."

—Brian Siebel, senior attorney for the Legal Action Project of the Brady Center to Prevent Gun Violence, November 2003

Most of these lawsuits have been won by the manufacturers. However, defending oneself in court is extremely expensive. The National Shooting Sports Foundation estimates that the firearms industry has spent more than $100 million defending itself in court. In 2003, gun rights supporters introduced a bill in Congress, the Protection of Lawful Commerce in Arms Act, to bar this type of lawsuit. If the bill passes, no one will be allowed to sue a gun maker for injury or death caused by a firearm.

GUN LAWS AROUND THE WORLD

In 2003, several international groups launched a campaign for an international arms trade treaty. They hope to collect a million or more signatures from around the world. The petition will be presented to the United Nations and will request that body to draft a treaty to regulate trade in handguns and other small arms. Some countries, such as Mexico, believe that the treaty should also deal with civilian ownership of firearms. The goal is to have the treaty signed by member countries in 2006. Japan, Great Britain, South Africa, Mexico, and Canada are among the nations supporting the treaty. The United States at present opposes the treaty unless it addresses only the international trade in firearms. If the treaty goes into effect, the nations signing it will have more uniform laws regulating the sale and possibly the use of guns.

DO FIREARMS LAWS WORK?

The United States has thousands of firearms laws intended to reduce gun violence. In 2003, the Centers for Disease Control and Prevention (CDC) studied the effect of those laws on rates of homicide and injury. The report said that there was not enough evidence to prove that U.S. gun laws are effective, nor was there enough evidence to show that gun laws are *not* effective. The CDC recommended further study.

Right now, international firearms laws are anything but uniform. In some countries, almost no private ownership of handguns is allowed. Other countries have much less strict laws. Here is a sampling of gun laws.

- **Australia:** Gun owners need a separate license for each handgun they own. Firearms are registered, and many types of semiautomatic rifles are prohibited.
- **Brazil:** In December 2003, Brazil passed what many consider to be the toughest gun laws in South America. Brazil's law, the Disarmament Act, allows only police, military, hunters, and licensed security guards to carry handguns. The minimum age for gun ownership is 25, and buyers must undergo a background check. The law also requires the government to hold a popular vote in 2005 about whether handguns should be banned completely in Brazil.
- **Canada:** Handguns must be registered, and some types are prohibited. Canadians need a Firearms Acquisition Certificate to buy a firearm. Semiautomatic rifles are strictly regulated.
- **Germany:** Licenses are required to buy or own a firearm, and applicants must prove that they need a gun and pass a test before a license is issued.
- **Great Britain:** Licenses are required for rifles, shotguns, and handguns. Semiautomatic rifles and all handguns except single-shot .22 calibers are prohibited. The NRA calls Britain's laws "a near ban on private ownership of firearms."
- **Israel:** A license is required to own any gun, but any law-abiding adult who has had firearms training can get a license. As Israelis routinely serve in the military, nearly all adults have had the necessary training.
- **Japan:** Rifles and handguns are prohibited. Shotguns are regulated strictly.
- **Luxembourg:** Guns are prohibited, except for military and law enforcement personnel.
- **Russia:** When Russia was part of the Soviet Union, the central government banned civilian handgun ownership. After the breakup of the Soviet Union, Russia and other countries passed their own laws. Almost no private citizen may own a handgun in Russia. Owners of shotguns and rifles must be licensed.

◆ **Switzerland:** Members of the military may keep their weapons at home when they are not on active duty. However, nonmilitary citizens of Switzerland need a permit for each purchase of a weapon. The Swiss Arms Act also requires a special permit to carry a firearm outside the home. Permits are given only to those who can demonstrate the need to carry a gun and who have passed a firearms safety course.

When the founders of the United States sat down in Philadelphia more than 200 years ago to guarantee "life, liberty, and the pursuit of happiness" to citizens, they probably did not imagine that terrorism, assault weapons, and rapid international travel would be considerations for their descendants. As the Second and Third Amendments enter their third century of existence, the courts, the government, and private individuals will continue to argue about the meaning and best application of these important statements.

Glossary

amendment   A change to the U.S. Constitution.

armor-piercing bullets   Specially designed bullets that can pass through a bulletproof vest.

Articles of Confederation   The document creating the first government of the United States. The Articles of Confederation failed because the central government had too little power and the states were too loosely organized.

assault weapons   Powerful, military-style firearms, often semiautomatic rifles.

automatic weapon   A gun that fires many bullets with one squeeze of the trigger.

ballistic fingerprinting   The practice of firing a gun before it is sold and keeping a record of the pattern on the bullet. Because each gun produces a unique pattern, law officers can match a bullet to the weapon that fired it.

biathlon   A shooting sport in which skiers follow a course and stop at certain places to target shoot.

Bill of Rights   The first 10 amendments to the Constitution that guarantee some basic American rights, including the right to bear arms and the right to be free from forced quartering.

bootlegger   Manufacturer or seller of illegal alcoholic beverages.

Brady Bill   Legislation passed in 1993 that requires background checks of purchasers of firearms and related regulation of firearms. The law bears the name of James Brady, press secretary to President Ronald Reagan. Both Brady and Reagan were wounded in an assassination attempt.

Brady Campaign to Prevent Gun Violence   An organization that works for stricter gun control laws.

Bureau of Alcohol, Tobacco, Firearms, and Explosives (ATF)   The federal agency charged with enforcing federal law regarding gun use and ownership.

burglary   A crime in which a criminal enters a home armed with a weapon.

child access protection laws (CAP laws)   Laws that describe how a gun must be stored so that it does not fall into the hands of children.

circuit courts of appeals   The level of the federal justice system immediately below the Supreme Court, the highest court in the nation. There are 12 judicial circuits in the United States, whose court of appeals hears cases ruled by its respective district courts and cases involving federal agencies.

common law   Established legal principles based on custom and precedent.

concealed carry laws   Laws that regulate when and how a citizen may carry a handgun outside the home.

federal government, U.S.   The central government of the United States, based in Washington, D.C.

Federalists   In early U.S. history, supporters of a strong central government. During the Constitutional Convention, Federalists were opposed by states' righters, who wanted to limit the power of the central government.

.50-caliber rifle   An extremely powerful weapon capable of firing bullets great distances. With special ammunition, a .50-caliber rifle bullet can go through thick steel.

fyrd   A Saxon militia. *Fyrds*, made up of adult men of each community, defended their families and homes when danger threatened.

gangsters   Violent criminals who are organized into a gang.

gun shows   Temporary markets where dealers and private individuals may buy and sell firearms. Some of the rules on background checks do not apply to the private sellers at gun shows.

Handgun Control, Inc.   An organization that fought for stricter gun control laws. It was renamed the Brady Campaign to Prevent Gun Violence in 2001.

individual rights view   An interpretation of the Second Amendment that sees the right to keep and bear arms as belonging to individual citizens.

interstate commerce   Trade or movement of goods between states. Congress has the power to regulate interstate commerce. Since most guns are sold across state lines, Congress often relies on its commerce power to pass gun control laws.

lobbyist   A person who tries to convince public officials of a particular point of view.

magazine   Ammunition cartridge.

militia   A fighting force drawn from a state or community. Militia members often serve only in times of emergency.

militia view   An interpretation of the Second Amendment that sees the right to keep and bear arms as belonging to the states. The states use that right to maintain militias.

muster   A militia drill, often with firearms.

National Guard   A military group maintained by each state. Some people see National Guards as modern-day militias.

National Rifle Association (NRA)   An organization that works for the right of every law-abiding adult American to own, carry, and use a gun.

quartering   The practice of providing food and shelter to troops by private citizens or local governments.

ratification   Acceptance of a new constitution or law.

redcoats   British soldiers who fought against the colonists in the Revolutionary War.

registration   When referring to firearms, registration is the practice of keeping track of the serial number and sale of each gun.

Saturday night specials   Cheap, inaccurate handguns that are often involved in crimes.

sawed-off shotguns   Shotguns with shortened barrels that can easily be hidden.

semiautomatic   Any firearm that automatically loads a bullet into the firing chamber with each squeeze of the trigger.

shotgun   A weapon that sprays tiny pellets, or shot, when it is fired.

smart gun   A firearm that will not fire for anyone other than the owner.

standing army   An army of professional soldiers that exists during both peace and war time.

states' righters   Opponents of a strong central government. States' righters favor giving maximum power to individual states.

tommy gun   A powerful semiautomatic rifle capable of firing 800 bullets per minute.

Tories   Colonists loyal to Britain and opposed to American independence.

waiting period   A period of time (originally five days) between the date when a buyer purchases a gun and when he or she takes possession of the weapon.

wheelock   The first gun to ignite gunpowder with a spark.

Chronology

fifth–11th centuries

- Saxons rule England and maintain local militias called *fyrds*.

ninth century (circa 871)

- King Alfred the Great of England requires able-bodied citizens to arm themselves at their own expense.

1066

- Normans conquer England. Nobles are required to equip and train knights for local defense. The king also maintains a group of knights to defend the throne, a royal standing army.

12th century

- Towns in England begin to negotiate charters guaranteeing certain rights, including the right to be free from forced quartering.

1130

- First official ban on forced quartering is enacted in the charter of the city of London.

1181

- Henry II orders every freeman to own a weapon, in case the king needs to call out the militia. The number and type of weapons varies according to the citizen's station in life.

1285

◆ During the reign of English king Edward I, the Statute of Winchester requires subjects to equip themselves with weapons for the defense of the state.

1328

◆ The Statute of Northampton states that no Englishman carry arms in public in a way that frightens ordinary citizens.

1383

◆ Richard II of England orders his subjects not to carry arms while riding.

1511

◆ English king Henry VIII commands his subjects to possess and train with longbows.

1514

◆ Henry VIII regulates which types of weapons may be owned and used. In general, wealthier English citizens may possess more and better-quality weapons.

1553

◆ Edward VI, king of England and Ireland, commands "all persons who shoot guns" to register with the local justice of the peace.

1619

◆ In Jamestown (Virginia), the law prohibits settlers from selling guns to Native Americans.

1623

◆ The Plymouth Colony (in Massachusetts) passes a law requiring freemen of the colony to have defensive weapons.

1628

◆ Parliament sends a list of grievances to the king, including the practice of forced quartering.

1640

◆ The colony of Virginia passes a law preventing African Americans from bearing arms.

1641

◆ The English government forbids the trade of firearms with Native Americans in the colonies.

1642

◆ Parliament passes the Militia Ordinance, giving itself control over the militias in England even if the king objects.

1645

◆ Oliver Cromwell, a brief civilian ruler of England, Scotland, and Ireland, creates a standing army.

1660–61

◆ Charles II of Great Britain and Ireland signs the Militia Act, placing local militias under royal control. Militias thought likely to rebel are dismantled. Various royal decrees limit access to weapons for ordinary citizens.

1671

◆ The Game Act restricts ownership of firearms in Great Britain. Those whose land is worth less than 100 pounds may not possess guns.

1674

◆ Major Edmund Andros, the British governor of New York, gathers all firearms and forbids Dutch residents access to these weapons.

1679

◆ Parliament passes the Anti-Quartering Act, which prohibits troops from being quartered in private homes in both peace and wartime.

1685

◆ James II comes to the throne of Great Britain and Ireland and continues to tighten royal control by disbanding militias and increasing the power of the standing army.

1689

◆ Newly crowned William and Mary of England are presented with the Declaration of Rights, which they accept to issue as law in order to gain the throne. Included in the Declaration of Rights is a statement saying the rulers will not create or keep a standing army without the consent of Parliament. The Declaration of Rights also guarantees the right to bear arms to Protestants.

1692

◆ The Massachusetts Bay Colony prohibits private citizens from carrying guns in public.

1723

◆ The colony of Virginia forbids African Americans and American Indians to own guns.

1756

◆ The colony of Maryland forbids Catholics to own guns.

1765

◆ Sir William Blackstone, an English political philosopher and historian, calls the right to bear arms one "of the absolute rights of individuals."

1774

◆ The British pass a law that allows troops to be quartered in private homes without the consent of the owner. This law outrages colonists in British North America.
◆ The first Continental Congress meets in Philadelphia, Pennsylvania. The congress urges colonies to form new militias not loyal to the British Crown.

1775

◆ The Battle of Lexington and Concord marks the beginning of the Revolutionary War. Fighting breaks out because British soldiers are ordered to destroy firearms and arrest militia leaders.

1776

◆ The Declaration of Independence is signed.

1777

◆ The Articles of Confederation are drawn up and sent to the states for comment and approval.

1781

◆ The Articles of Confederation go into effect. Every state must keep an armed militia. No national army is provided for.

1787

◆ A Constitutional Convention is held in Philadelphia. The delegates discuss the role of a militia, standing army, quartering, and the right to bear arms. The Constitution is drafted.

1789

◆ The U.S. Constitution replaces the Articles of Confederation as the supreme law of the United States.

1791

◆ The Bill of Rights amends the Constitution and guarantees "the right to keep and bear arms" and the right to be free from forced quartering to Americans.

1792

◆ The Uniform Militia Act creates standards for state militias. Militia members must be between 18 and 45 years of age. Slaves, freed blacks, and Native Americans may not be members of the militia.

19th century

◆ In the United States, some states and towns pass laws restricting gun ownership and use. No federal laws regulate firearms during this period.

1808

◆ The federal government distributes arms and ammunition to state militias, which are now called "national guards."

1876

◆ In *United States v. Cruikshank,* the Supreme Court rules that the Second Amendment limits the power of the federal government, not the powers of the states.

1886

◆ The Supreme Court rules in *Presser v. Illinois* that the Second Amendment does not limit the power of the state to regulate military associations and parades by armed private soldiers. The Court also defines militia as all citizens of the United States capable of bearing arms.

1894

◆ In *Miller v. Texas,* the Supreme Court writes that the Second Amendment applies only to the federal government and does not limit the powers of the states.

1919

◆ The Volstead Act, the Eighteenth Amendment, prohibits alcoholic beverages in the United States. Gangsters begin to sell alcohol, and the crime rate rises.

1921

◆ The tommy gun, a powerful rifle capable of firing 800 bullets per minute, is invented.

1922

◆ The Committee on Law Enforcement of the American Bar Association, a lawyers' organization, calls for a ban on the manufacture and sale of pistols except for government use.

1927

◆ Congress bans the sending of firearms through the U.S. postal system with the Miller Act. Gun manufacturers switch to private shipping companies.

1934

◆ The National Firearms Act places a high tax on the manufacture, sale, and purchase of machine guns and sawed-off shotguns.

1938

◆ The Federal Firearms Act requires a license for gun manufacturers and dealers who ship their products across state lines. Firearms may not be sold to those convicted of serious crimes.

1939

◆ In *U.S. v. Miller* the Supreme Court rules that in banning sawed-off shotguns, the National Firearms Act does not violate the Constitution.

1963

◆ President John F. Kennedy is assassinated. Afterward, 17 gun control bills are introduced in Congress, and 170 bills are proposed on the state level.

1968

◆ *April:* Reverend Martin Luther King, Jr., is assassinated.
◆ *June:* Robert Kennedy is assassinated.
◆ *June:* The Omnibus Crime Control and Safe Streets Act replaces the Federal Firearms Act. Pistols and revolvers may not be shipped across state lines to private individuals. No one may buy a handgun outside his or her home state.
◆ *October:* The Gun Control Act is passed. This law raises license fees and creates strict licensing rules for dealers who ship across state lines or to other countries. Military weapons and cheap handguns (Saturday night specials) may not be imported. No firearms may be sold to minors, mentally disabled people, or convicted criminals. The law also gives extra penalties for crimes committed with firearms.

1972

◆ The Bureau of Alcohol, Tobacco, and Firearms is created and charged with enforcing gun laws.

1974

◆ The National Council to Control Handguns is established. This group works for stricter regulation of handguns. In 1980, it is renamed Handgun Control, Inc.

1980

◆ *Lewis v. United States* is heard by the Supreme Court, which rules that it is constitutional to bar the right to bear arms to anyone convicted of a serious crime.

1982

- *Engblom v. Carey,* the only Third Amendment case to reach the courts, is tried. The circuit court of appeals rules that prison guards who live in government housing may not be displaced in order to quarter troops.

1986

- Many types of armor-piercing ammunition are banned.
- The Firearms Owners' Protection Act is passed. This law changes some parts of the Gun Control Act of 1968. Penalties for gun crimes are again increased, but penalties for dealers who do not keep adequate records are decreased. Gun shows are allowed if the dealer is licensed in the state where the show is held. Rifles and shotguns may be sold across state lines as long as the sale does not violate the laws of either state.

1988

- The Undetectable Firearms Act is passed. It is illegal to make, import, or sell plastic guns that cannot be detected by metal detectors in airports.

1989

- President George H. W. Bush issues an executive order banning assault weapons.

1990

- The Gun Free School Zones Act makes it illegal to possess firearms in a school zone, whether or not the school is in session. The law is challenged in court, and the Supreme Court rules it unconstitutional.

1993

- The Brady Handgun Violence Prevention Act calls for a waiting period of seven days between purchase and possession of a handgun. The Brady Bill also bars those convicted of serious crime, drug users or sellers, those under court order for stalking, and the mentally ill from gun ownership.

1994

◆ The Violent Crime Control and Law Enforcement Act outlaws some types of assault weapons for a period of 10 years.

1995

◆ The Gun-Free Schools Act bans from school zones all firearms that have been shipped across state lines (nearly all weapons fit this category). It replaces the Gun Free School Zones Act of 1990, which was ruled unconstitutional.

1996

◆ Those convicted of domestic violence are legally barred from buying or owning a gun.

1998

◆ The waiting period between purchase and possession of a handgun as established by the 1993 Brady Handgun Violence Prevention Act is reduced to five days. Later in the year, the National Instant Check System, a computer program that performs background checks on gun buyers, is established, and the waiting period is no longer required.
◆ President Bill Clinton renews an executive order banning assault weapons that was first issued in 1989 by then-president George H. W. Bush.

1999

◆ Georgia becomes the first state to protect gun manufacturers from lawsuits. No city or county may sue a gun manufacturer for damages because a firearm was improperly used.

2000

◆ *March:* Smith and Wesson gun manufacturers agree to a code of conduct for sales of firearms. In return, many cities and counties withdraw their lawsuits against the company.
◆ *May:* The Million Mom March rallies in Washington, D.C., for stricter gun control.

2001

♦ Handgun Control, Inc., is renamed the Brady Campaign to Prevent Gun Violence.

2003

♦ In *NAACP v. Accusport Inc. et al,* a federal court rejects the argument of the National Association for the Advancement of Colored People (NAACP) that the group receive damages from gun manufacturers because many of their members have been harmed by firearms.

2004

♦ *September:* The assault weapons ban expires.

2005

♦ *January:* New York City Council passes the Gun Industry Responsibility Act, which gives victims of firearms crime the right to sue the manufacturer of the weapon. The law also says that gun violence victims may sue manufacturers that market products at guns shows where background checks are not performed.

Appendix

Excerpts from Documents Relating to the Right to Bear Arms and Not to Quarter Troops

Declaration of Independence, 1776

These statements contain American complaints about quartering and the maintenance of a standing army. *He* refers to the British king George III. *For* comes before each reason why the colonies must become independent of Britain.

He has kept among us, in Times of Peace, Standing Armies, without the consent of our Legislatures.

He has affected to render [make] the Military independent of and superior to the Civil Power.

. . .

For quartering large Bodies of Armed Troops among us;

For protecting them [British soldiers], by a mock Trial, from Punishment for any Murders which they should commit on the Inhabitants of these States.

121

Articles of Confederation, 1781

The Articles of Confederation established the first government of the United States. The articles did not address the right to keep and bear arms, but the document did discuss the rights of the state and federal government to keep armies and militias.

❧

Article VI. No vessels of war shall be kept up in time of peace by any State, except such number only, as shall be deemed necessary by the United States in Congress assembled, for the defence of such State, or its trade; nor shall any body of forces be kept up by any State, in time of peace, except such number only, as in the judgement of the United States, in Congress assembled, shall be deemed requisite to garrison the forts necessary for the defence of such State; but every State shall always keep up a well-regulated and disciplined militia, sufficiently armed and accoutred [outfitted], and shall provide and constantly have ready for use, in public stores, a due number of field pieces and tents, and a proper quantity of arms, ammunition and camp equipage [equipment].

Constitution of the United States, 1787

The U.S. Constitution established the form of government that now exists in the United States. The original document discussed neither the right to keep and bear arms nor the right to be free from forced quartering. These rights were provided for in the Bill of Rights. The Constitution did, however, address the role of a standing army and militia.

❧

ARTICLE I, SECTION 8

Clause 12: To raise and support Armies, but no Appropriation [allowance] of Money to that Use shall be for a longer Term than two Years;

Clause 13: To provide and maintain a Navy;

Clause 14: To make Rules for the Government and Regulation of the land and naval Forces;

Clause 15: To provide for calling forth the Militia to execute the Laws of the Union, suppress Insurrections and repel Invasions;

Clause 16: To provide for organizing, arming, and disciplining, the Militia, and for governing such Part of them as may be employed in the Service of the United States, reserving to the States respectively, the Appointment of the Officers, and the Authority of training the Militia according to the discipline prescribed by Congress; . . .

Bill of Rights, 1791

The Bill of Rights, the first 10 amendments to the U.S. Constitution, guaranteed Americans certain rights, including to keep and bear arms and to be free from forced quartering.

Second Amendment: A well regulated Militia, being necessary to the security of a free State, the right of the people to keep and bear Arms, shall not be infringed.

Third Amendment: No soldier shall, in time of peace be quartered in any house, without the consent of the Owner, nor in time of war, but in a manner to be prescribed by law.

Right to Bear Arms in State Constitutions

Six states do not provide for the right to bear arms in their constitutions: California, Iowa, Maryland, Minnesota, New Jersey, and New York. The other states' constitutions express the right in various ways.

Alabama: That every citizen has a right to bear arms in defense of himself and the state.

Alaska: A well-regulated militia being necessary to the security of a free state, the right of the people to keep and bear arms shall not be infringed [violated]. The individual right to keep and bear arms shall not be denied or infringed by the State or a political subdivision of the State.

Arizona: The right of the individual citizen to bear arms in defense of himself or the State shall not be impaired [damaged], but nothing in this section shall be construed [understood] as authorizing individuals or corporations to organize, maintain, or employ an armed body of men.

Arkansas: The citizens of this State shall have the right to keep and bear arms for their common defense.

Colorado: The right of no person to keep and bear arms in defense of his home, person and property, or in aid of the civil power when thereto legally summoned, shall be called in question; but nothing herein contained shall be construed to justify the practice of carrying concealed weapons.

Connecticut: Every citizen has a right to bear arms in defense of himself and the state.

Delaware: A person has the right to keep and bear arms for the defense of self, family, home and State, and for hunting and recreational use.

Florida: (a) The right of the people to keep and bear arms in defense of themselves and of the lawful authority of the state shall not be infringed [violated], except that the manner of bearing arms may be regulated by law.

(b) There shall be a mandatory period of three days, excluding weekdays and legal holidays, between the purchase and delivery at retail of any handgun. For the purposes of this section, "purchase" means the transfer of money or other valuable consideration to the retailer, and "handgun" means a firearm capable of being carried and used by one hand, such as a pistol or revolver. Holders of a concealed weapon permit as prescribed in Florida law shall not be subject to the provisions of this paragraph.

(c) The legislature shall enact legislation implementing [putting in place] subsection (b) of this section, effective no later than December 31, 1991, which shall provide that anyone violating the provisions of subsection (b) shall be guilty of a felony.

(d) This restriction shall not apply to a trade in of another handgun.

Georgia: The right of the people to keep and bear arms shall not be infringed [violated], but the General Assembly shall have power to prescribe the manner in which arms may be borne.

Hawaii: A well regulated militia being necessary to the security of a free state, the right of the people to keep and bear arms shall not be infringed [violated].

Idaho: The people have the right to keep and bear arms, which right shall not be abridged [limited]; but this provision shall not prevent the passage of laws to govern the carrying of weapons concealed on the person nor prevent passage of legislation providing minimum sentences for crimes committed while in possession of a firearm, nor prevent the passage of legislation providing penalties for the possession of firearms by a convicted felon, nor prevent the passage of any legislation punishing the use of a firearm. No law shall impose licensure, registration or special taxation on the ownership or possession of firearms or ammunition. Nor shall any law permit the confiscation [taking away] of firearms, except those actually used in the commission of a felony.

Illinois: Subject only to the police power, the right of the individual citizen to keep and bear arms shall not be infringed [violated].

Indiana: The people shall have a right to bear arms, for the defense of themselves and the State.

Kansas: The people have the right to bear arms for their defense and security; but standing armies, in time of peace, are dangerous to liberty, and shall not be tolerated, and the military shall be in strict subordination to the civil power.

Kentucky: All men are, by nature, free and equal, and have certain inherent [natural] and inalienable [not to be denied] rights, among which may be reckoned:

First: The right of enjoying and defending their lives and liberties. . . .

Seventh: The right to bear arms in defense of themselves and of the State, subject to the power of the General Assembly to enact laws to prevent persons from carrying concealed weapons.

Louisiana: The right of each citizen to keep and bear arms shall not be abridged [limited], but this provision shall not prevent the passage of laws to prohibit the carrying of weapons concealed on the person.

Maine: Every citizen has a right to keep and bear arms and this right shall never be questioned.

Massachusetts: The people have a right to keep and to bear arms for the common defence. And as, in time of peace, armies are dangerous to liberty, they ought not to be maintained without the consent of the legislature; and the military power shall always be held in an exact subordination to the civil authority, and be governed by it.

Michigan: Every person has a right to keep and bear arms for the defense of himself and the state.

Mississippi: The right of every citizen to keep and bear arms in defense of his home, person, or property, or in aid of the civil power when thereto legally summoned, shall not be called in question, but the legislature may regulate or forbid carrying concealed weapons.

Missouri: That the right of every citizen to keep and bear arms in defense of his home, person and property, or when lawfully summoned in aid of the civil power, shall not be questioned; but this shall not justify the wearing of concealed weapons.

Montana: The right of any person to keep or bear arms in defense of his own home, person, and property, or in aid of the civil power when thereto legally summoned, shall not be called in question, but nothing herein contained shall be held to permit the carrying of concealed weapons.

Nebraska: All persons are by nature free and independent, and have certain inherent [natural] and inalienable [not to be denied] rights; among these are life, liberty, the pursuit of happiness, and the right to keep and bear arms for security or defense of self, family, home, and others, and for lawful common defense, hunting, recreational use, and all other lawful purposes, and such rights shall not be denied or infringed [violated] by the state or any subdivision thereof. To secure these rights, and the protection of property, governments are instituted among people, deriving their just powers from the consent of the governed.

Nevada: Every citizen has the right to keep and bear arms for security and defense, for lawful hunting and recreational use and for other lawful purposes.

New Hampshire: All persons have the right to keep and bear arms in defense of themselves, their families, their property and the state.

New Mexico: No law shall abridge the right of the citizen to keep and bear arms for security and defense, for lawful hunting and recreational use and for other lawful purposes, but nothing herein shall be held to permit the carrying of concealed weapons. No municipality or county shall regulate, in any way, an incident of the right to keep and bear arms.

North Carolina: A well regulated militia being necessary to the security of a free State, the right of the people to keep and bear arms shall not be infringed [violated]; and, as standing armies in time of peace are dangerous to liberty, they shall not be maintained, and the military shall be kept under strict subordination to, and governed by, the civil power. Nothing herein shall justify the practice of carrying concealed weapons, or prevent the General Assembly from enacting penal statutes against that practice.

North Dakota: All individuals are by nature equally free and independent and have certain inalienable [not to be denied] rights, among which are those of enjoying and defending life and liberty; acquiring, possessing and protecting property and reputation; pursuing and obtaining safety and happiness; and to keep and bear arms for the defense of their person, family, property, and the state, and for lawful hunting, recreational, and other lawful purposes, which shall not be infringed [violated].

Ohio: The people have the right to bear arms for their defense and security; but standing armies, in time of peace, are dangerous to liberty, and shall not be kept up; and the military shall be in strict subordination to the civil power.

Oklahoma: The right of a citizen to keep and bear arms in defense of his home, person, or property, or in aid of the civil power, when thereunto legally summoned, shall never be prohibited; but nothing herein contained shall prevent the Legislature from regulating the carrying of weapons.

Oregon: The people shall have the right to bear arms for the defence of themselves, and the State, but the Military shall be kept in strict subordination to the civil power.

Pennsylvania: The right of the citizens to bear arms in defence of themselves and the State shall not be questioned.

Rhode Island: The right of the people to keep and bear arms shall not be infringed [violated].

South Carolina: A well regulated militia being necessary to the security of a free State, the right of the people to keep and bear arms shall not be infringed [violated]. As, in times of peace, armies are dangerous to liberty, they shall not be maintained without the consent of the General Assembly. The military power of the State shall always be held in subordination to the civil authority and be governed by it.

South Dakota: The right of the citizens to bear arms in defense of themselves and the state shall not be denied.

Tennessee: That the citizens of this State have a right to keep and to bear arms for their common defense; but the Legislature shall have power, by law, to regulate the wearing of arms with a view to prevent crime.

Texas: Every citizen shall have the right to keep and bear arms in the lawful defense of himself or the State; but the Legislature shall have power, by law, to regulate the wearing of arms, with a view to prevent crime.

Utah: The individual right of the people to keep and bear arms for security and defense of self, family, others, property, or the state, as well as for other lawful purposes shall not be infringed [violated]; but nothing herein shall prevent the legislature from defining the lawful use of arms.

Vermont: That the people have a right to bear arms for the defence of themselves and the State—and as standing armies in time of peace are dangerous to liberty, they ought not to be kept up; and that the military should be kept under strict subordination to and governed by the civil power.

Virginia: That a well regulated militia, composed of the body of the people, trained to arms, is the proper, natural, and safe defense of a free state, therefore, the right of the people to keep and bear arms shall not be infringed [violated]; that standing armies, in time of peace, should be avoided as dangerous to liberty; and that in all cases the military should be under strict subordination to, and governed by, the civil power.

Washington: The right of the individual citizen to bear arms in defense of himself, or the state, shall not be impaired [damaged], but nothing in this section shall be construed [understood] as authorizing individuals or corporations to organize, maintain or employ an armed body of men.

West Virginia: A person has the right to keep and bear arms for the defense of self, family, home and state, and for lawful hunting and recreational use.

Wisconsin: The people have the right to keep and bear arms for security, defense, hunting, recreation or any other lawful purpose.

Wyoming: The right of citizens to bear arms in defense of themselves and of the state shall not be denied.

Further Reading

Aitkens, Maggie. *Should We Have Gun Control?* Minneapolis, Minn.: Lerner, 1992.

Bijlefeld, Marjolijn. *The Gun Control Debate: A Documentary History.* Westport, Conn.: Greenwood Publishing, 1997.

Cothran, Helen, ed. *Gun Control: Opposing Viewpoints.* San Diego, Calif.: Greenhaven, 2002.

Currie-McGhee, Leanne K. *Gun Control.* San Diego, Calif.: Lucent, 2004.

Henderson, Harry. *Gun Control.* New York: Facts On File, 2000.

Long, Barbara. *Gun Control and the Right to Bear Arms: A Pro/Con Issue.* Berkeley Heights, N.J.: Enslow Publishers, 2002.

Lunger, Norman L. *Big Bang: The Loud Debate over Gun Control.* New York: 21st Century Books, 2002.

Siegel, Mark, Mei Ling Rein, and Nancy R. Jacobs, eds. *Gun Control: An American Issue.* 3d ed. Detroit, Mich.: Information Plus, 1997.

Streissguth, Thomas. *Gun Control: The Pros and Cons.* Berkeley Heights, N.J.: Enslow Publishers, 2001.

Valdez, Angela, and Alan Marzilli, eds. *Gun Control: Point-Counterpoint.* Broomall, Pa.: Chelsea House, 2003.

Bibliography

Books

Amar, Akhil Reed. *The Bill of Rights.* New Haven, Conn.: Yale University Press, 1998.

Brown, Peter Harry, and Daniel G. Abel. *Outgunned.* New York: Free Press, 2003.

Carter, Gregg Lee. *The Gun Control Movement.* New York: Twayne, 1997.

Cook, Philip, and Jens Ludwig. *Evaluating Gun Policy.* Washington, D.C.: Brookings Institution Press, 2003.

Davidson, Osha Gray. *Under Fire: The NRA and the Battle for Gun Control.* New York: Henry Holt, 1993.

DeConde, Alexander. *Gun Violence in America.* Boston: Northeastern University Press, 2001.

Gottfried, Ted. *Gun Control.* Brookfield, Conn.: Millbrook Press, 1993.

Krug, E. G., K. E. Powell, and L. Dahlberg. *Firearms Mortality in 36 Countries.* Atlanta, Ga.: Centers for Disease Control, 1993.

Nisbet, Lee, ed. *The Gun Control Debate.* Amherst, N.Y.: Prometheus Press, 2001.

Quiran, Jacquelyn. *Gun Control: An American Issue.* Detroit, Mich.: Gale Group, 2001.

Torr, James D. *Gun Violence: Opposing Viewpoints.* San Diego, Calif.: Greenhaven Press, 2002.

Articles

Amfire. "Police Cannot Protect and Are Not Required to Protect Every Individual." Available online. URL: http://www.amfire.com/factsheet/htm. Downloaded on October 18, 2003.

Bell, Tom W. "The Third Amendment: Forgotten but Not Gone." Available online. URL: http://www.tomwbell.com/writings/3rd.html. Downloaded on June 5, 2003.

Berger, Loren, and Dennis Henigan. "Guns and Terror." Brady Center to Prevent Gun Violence. Available online. URL: http://www.gunlawsuits.org/downloads/guns&terror. Downloaded on January 28, 2004.

Brady Campaign to Prevent Gun Violence. "Brady Campaign Says Congress' Anti-Terrorism Legislation Should Have Tightened Nation's Gun Laws." Available online. URL: http://www.bradycampaign.org/press/release.asp. Downloaded on January 8, 2003.

———. "Destruction of Background Check Records." Available online. URL: http://www.bradycampaign.org/legislation/federal/omnibus. Downloaded on January 9, 2004.

———. "House Passes Appropriations Provisions That Undermine Law Enforcement Efforts to Stop Gun Crimes and Fight Terrorism." Available online. URL: http://www.bradycampaign.org/press/release.asp. Downloaded on January 9, 2004.

———. "Indiana Supreme Court Gives Green Light to Gary, Indiana's Lawsuit Against Gun Industry." Available online. URL: http://www.bradycampaign.org/press/release.asp. Downloaded on January 9, 2004.

———. "Selling High-Powered Military Weapons in the Suburbs." Available online. URL: http://www.bradycampaign.org/facts/issuebriefs. Downloaded on January 9, 2004.

Brookings Institution. "Do Guns Deter Burglars?" Available online. URL: http://www.jointogether.org/gv/news/summaries. Downloaded on November 19, 2003.

Bureau of Justice Statistics. "After Falling to Levels Last Experienced in the 1980's, the Number of Crimes Committed with Firearms Stabilized in 2001." Available online. URL: http://www.ojp.usdoj.gov/bjs. Downloaded on October 28, 2003.

———. "Firearms and Crime Statistics." Available online. URL: http://www.ojp.usdoj.gov/bjs/guns/htm. Downloaded on October 10, 2003.

———. "Weapon Use and Violent Crime." Available online. URL: http://www.ojp.usdoj.gov/bjs/abstract/wuvc01.htm. Downloaded on October 10, 2003.

Butterfield, Fox. "Rate of Serious Crime Held Largely Steady Last Year, Report by FBI Says." *New York Times,* October 28, 2003, A16.

ChildTrends Databank. "Teen Homicide, Suicide, and Firearm Death." Available online. URL: http://www.childtrendsdatabank.org/indicators/70ViolentDeath.cfm. Downloaded on November 18, 2003.

Committee on the Judiciary of the U.S. Senate, 97th Congress. "The Right to Keep and Bear Arms." Washington, D.C.: Government Printing Office, 1982.

Dahl, Dick. "CDC Report Highlights Need for Better Research." *Join Together.* Available online. URL: http://www.jointogether.org. Downloaded on November 19, 2003.

"Deal Struck on Gun Buyer Data." *Washington Post,* November 26, 2003. Available online. URL: http://www.washingtonpost.com. Downloaded on January 9, 2004.

Delo, Howard. "Outdoors in Alaska." *Frontiersman.* Available online. URL: http://www.frontiersman.com/articles/2003/10/20/news/opinion. Downloaded on December 2, 2003.

Dewan, Shaila K. "In the Fact of Death, an Undercover Life of Guns." *New York Times,* October 5, 2003. A1.

Eggen, Dan. "FBI Curbed in Tracking Gun Buyers." *Washington Post,* November 18, 2003. Available online. URL: http://www.washingtonpost.com. Downloaded on January 9, 2004.

———. "FBI Gets More Time on Gun Buys." Washington Post, November 22, 2003. Available online. URL: http://www.washingtonpost.com. Downloaded on January 9, 2004.

Federal Bureau of Investigation, U.S. Department of Justice. "Law Enforcement Officers Killed and Assaulted in 2002." May 12, 2003. Available online. URL: http://www.fbi.gov. Downloaded on November 19, 2003.

Fields, William S., and David T. Hardy. "The Third Amendment and the Issue of the Maintenance of Standing Armies: A Legal History." *American Journal of Legal History* 35 (1991): 393.

Freeman, Jennifer. "Gun Control or Gun Safety: What's the Difference?" *Sierra Times,* October 15, 2003. Available online. URL: http://www.sierratimes.com. Downloaded on December 2, 2003.

Glaberson, William. "Gun Makers Repel Lawsuit by NAACP." *New York Times,* July 22, 2003, B1.

Green, Sara Jean. "Needed: A Pair of Track Shoes, a Steady Hand—Athletes Compete in Biathlon." *Seattle Times,* June 26, 2000, B3.

Guart, Al. "NYers Going Ballistic." *New York Post,* August 10, 2003, 8.

Hemenway, D., and M. Miller. "Association of Rates of Household Handgun Ownership, Lifetime Major Depression, and Serious Suicidal Thoughts with Rates of Suicide Across U.S. Census Regions." *Injury Prevention* 8, no. 4 (2002): 313–316.

Japanese Mission to the EU. "Firearms Regulations and Public Safety." Available online. URL: http://www.eu.emb-japan.go.jp/interest/firearms.htm. Downloaded on December 8, 2003.

Jeter, Jon. "Brazil Passes Tough Gun-Control Laws." *Washington Post,* December 24, 2003, A12.

Join Together Online. "Guns Responsible for 51 of 56 Police Deaths." Available online. URL: http://www.jointogether.org/gv/news/summaries. Downloaded on November 19, 2003.

Kellerman, Al. "Injuries and Deaths Due to Firearms in the Home." *Journal of Trauma* 45, no. 2 (1998): 263–267.

Kristof, Nicholas D. "Japanese Say No to Crime: Tough Methods, at a Price." *New York Times,* May 4, 1995, pp. 1–2.

———. "One Nation Bars, the Other Requires." *New York Times,* March 10, 1996, section 4, p. 3.

Krouse, William. "Foreign Terrorists and the Availability of Firearms and Black Powder in the United States." *Congressional Research Service,* May 16, 2003, pp. 1–10.

Lichtblau, Eric. "50% of Dealers Willing to Sell Handguns Illegally, Study Says." *New York Times,* June 17, 2003, A19.

Lies, Elaine. "Japan Suicide Rate Clings Near Record High." *Corporate Watch in Japanese,* June 30, 2000. Available online. URL: http://www.jca.apc.org/web-news/corpwatch-jp;/47.html. Downloaded on December 8, 2003.

Ludwig, Jens, and Philip J. Cook. "Homicide and Suicide Rates Associated with Implementation of the Brady Handgun Violence Prevention Act." *Journal of the American Medical Association,* August 2, 2000. Available online. URL: http://www.jama.ama-assn.org/cgi/content/abstract/284/5/585. Downloaded on December 5, 2003.

McIntire, Mike. "Differing Views Are Voiced by City on Gun Lawsuits." *New York Times,* September 13, 2003, B4.

Minino, A., et al. "Deaths: Final Data for 2000." *National Vital Statistics Reports* 50, no. 15 (2002): 44.

National Center for Health Statistics. "Firearm Mortality." Available online. URL: http://www.cdc.gov/nchs/fastats/firearms.htm. Downloaded on October 10, 2003.

National Center for Injury Prevention and Control. "Facts on Adolescent Injury." Available online. URL: http://www.cdc.gov/ncipc/factsheets/adoles.htm. Downloaded on December 5, 2003.

————. "Fatal Firearms Injuries in the United States, 1962–1994." *Violence Surveillance Summary* Series, No. 3. Available online. URL: http://www.cdc.gov/ncipc/pub-res/firearmsu.htm. Downloaded on December 5, 2003.

National Institute of Child Health and Human Development. "Major Causes of Early Childhood Death from Injury Identified." *NIH News Alert.* Available online. URL: http://www.nichd.nih.gov/new/releases/deaths2.cfm. Downloaded on December 8, 2003.

National Rifle Association. "Australia's Gun Ban, Crime and Video Tape." Available online. URL: http://www.nraila.org/Issues/FactSheets/Read. Downloaded on December 2, 2003.

————. "It's Not Just Gun Control Laws." Available online. URL: http://www.nraila.org/Issues/FactSheets/Read. Downloaded on December 2, 2003.

————. "Legacy." Available online. URL: http://www.nrahq.org/law/index.asp. Downloaded on October 31, 2003.

————. "NRA-ILA Firearms Facts." Available online. URL: http://www.nraila.org/FactSheets.asp. Downloaded on September 24, 2003.

————. "NRA-ILA Hunting Facts." Available online. URL: http://www.nraila.org/FactSheets.asp. Downloaded on October 10, 2003.

————. "Remarks by Governor Jeb Bush at 2003 NRA Annual Meeting." Available online. URL: http://www.nraila.org/News/Read/Speeches. Downloaded on January 9, 2004.

————. "Suicide and Firearms." Available online. URL: http://www.nraila.org/FactSheets. Downloaded on September 24, 2003.

————. "The War Against Handguns." Available online. URL: http://www.nraila.org/FactSheets.asp. Downloaded on September 24, 2003.

New York City Police Department. "Getting Guns Off the Streets." Available online. URL: http://www.ojjdp.ncjrs.org/pubs/gun_violence. Downloaded on November 20, 2003.

"Number of Deaths from Injury by Firearms." National Vital Statistics Report 50, no. 15 (September 16, 2002): 69.

Rother, Larry. "Brazil Adopts Strict Gun Control to Try to Curb Murders." *New York Times,* January 21, 2004, A3.

Smith, Tom W. "Statistics on Public Opinion on Gun Control." 1999. National Opinion Research Center of the University of Chicago. Available online. URL: http://www.norc.uchicago.edu/online/gunrpt. Downloaded on January 28, 2004.

Violence Policy Center. "Who Dies? A Look at Firearms Death and Injury in America—Revised Edition." Available online. URL: http://www.vpc.org/studies/whointro.htm. Downloaded on November 18, 2003.

Wharton, Tom, and Brett Prettyman. "Changing Laws, Views Have Hunters Turning Out in Fewer Numbers." *Salt Lake Tribune*, October 13, 2003. Available online. URL: http://www.sltrib.com/2003/Oct/10132003. Downloaded on November 4, 2003.

Wiebe, D. "Homicide and Suicide Risks Associated with Firearms in the Home: A National Case-Control Study." *Annals of Emergency Medicine* 41, no. 6 (June 2003): 771–782.

Index

Page numbers in *italic* indicate photographs. Page numbers in **boldface** indicate box features and margin quotations. Page numbers followed by *m* indicate maps. Page numbers followed by *t* indicate tables or graphs. Page numbers followed by *g* indicate glossary entries. Page numbers followed by *c* indicate chronology entries.

A

accidents
  children 77
  deaths (2000) 71–72
  Eddie Eagle GunSafe Program **90**
  gun control opponents' view of 89–90
  gun fatalities 90
advocacy groups
  anti–gun control 91–93
  pro–gun control 83–84
African Americans
  colonial gun laws 12, 113*c*
  Dred Scott v. Sandford 86
  gun prohibition in colonial Virginia 113*c*, 114*c*
  NAACP v. Accusport Inc. et al 60, 120*c*
  Uniform Militia Act 115*c*
  United States v. Cruikshank 47
age, for gun purchases 35, **73**
aggravated assaults 69
airport security checks 94
air rifles 65
AK-47 assault rifle 37, 58, 96
Alabama state constitution 123
Alaska state constitution 123

Alfred the Great (king of England) 6–7, 111*c*
"all citizens capable of bearing arms" 50
amendment 107*g*
American Bar Association Committee on Law Enforcement 116*c*
American colonies (1763) 14*m*
American Firearms Association 88
American Firearms Industry Magazine (Web site) 62
American Hunter magazine 65
American Indians. *See* Native Americans
American Revolution 18, 19–29
ammunition 35, 36, 54–55, **63,** 118*c*
Andros, Edmund 13, 113*c*
anti-Federalists 28. *See also* states' righters/states' rights
Anti-Quartering Act (England) 6, 113*c*
appeals, Supreme Court and 45
Arizona 54, 123–124
Arkansas 60, 124
arming of citizens, mandatory 111*c*
armor-piercing bullets 35, 107*g*, 118*c*

army, professional 4
Article I (U.S. Constitution) 22
Articles of Confederation 20–21, 107*g*, 115*c*, 122
Ashcroft, John 101, *102*
assassinations 34–35, 78–79, 78*t*, 117*c*
assault weapons 107*g*
  ban 118*c*, 120*c*
  current issues 100–101
  executive orders on assault weapons 37, 119*c*
  Great Britain 105
  Tanya Metaksa on ban **36**
  Ronald Reagan on ban **37**
  Silveira v. Lockyer 58–59
  terrorists 95, 96
  Violent Crime Control and Law Enforcement Act 37, 40, 119*c*
Australian gun control laws 105
automatic weapon **63,** 107*g*
automobiles 82–83, 86–87, 90

B

background checks
  Brady Bill 38
  during Bush administration 101

during Clinton administration 101
destruction of records 97
Disarmament Act (Brazil) 105
Gun Industry Responsibility Act 120c
improvement of **98**
National Firearms Act 33
National Instant Check System 119c
Printz v. United States 53–54
public opinion **73**
resale of guns **73**
suspected terrorists 97, 99
waiting period 82
ballistic fingerprinting **100,** 107g
ballistics records **100**
barrel **63**
Bean, Thomas Lamar 54–55
Beverly, Robert **11**
biathlon **65,** 107g
Bill of Rights ix, x, 25, 27–29, 107g, 123
Declaration of Rights and 6
ratification 24, 115c
Second Amendment's importance 85
billy club 61
blackjack 60
Blackstone, Sir William **8**
Blanton, Thomas **32**
bombs 33, 60
bootlegger 107g
box cutters 96
Brady, James 38, *39*, **39,** *54,* 76, 83
Brady, Sarah 38, *39*, **39,** 83
Brady Bill 107g. *See also* Brady Handgun Violence Prevention Act of 1993
Brady Campaign to Prevent Gun Violence 82–84, 103, 108g, 120c
Brady Center to Prevent Gun Violence **39**
Brady Handgun Violence Prevention Act of 1993 (Brady Bill) 38, 40, *54,* 118c
background checks 82, **98**
James and Sarah Brady **39**
Printz v. United States 53–54
suicide rates 89
waiting period 119c
Brazilian gun control laws 105
British army. *See* redcoats
Brookings Institution 67, 69, **76**
Brooklyn, New York 60

Bryan, Samuel 23
bulletproof vest 35
Bureau of Alcohol, Tobacco, Firearms, and Explosives (ATF) 108g
creation of 117c
Federal Firearms Transaction Record 97
firearm dealers' inventory 99
handguns purchased in South 79
United States v. Bean 55
Bureau of Justice Statistics 70t, 71t
burglary 67, 77, 108g
Bush, George H. W. 37, 118c
Bush, George W. 40, **96,** 101
Bush, Jeb **96,** 103

C

California 58–59
Canada 87, 104, 105
canceling, of gun permits 88
car crash fatalities, gun fatalities vs. 90
Carey, Hugh 61
Catholics 7, 12, 114c
Centers for Disease Control and Prevention (CDC)
accidental shootings (2000) 71–72
firearms deaths of youth in United States 76
studies on effect of gun laws **104**
suicides and firearms (2001) 73
Center to Prevent Handgun Violence **39,** 83
Centralia, Illinois **39**
Charles II (king of England) 2, 3, 4, 113c
charters 111c
checking system, computerized. *See* computerized checking system
Chicago, Illinois 48
child access protection laws (CAP laws) 43, 44m, 108g
children. *See* young people
circuit courts of appeals **55,** 55–60, 108g
Citizens' Committee for the Right to Keep and Bear Arms 92–93
citizenship, and right to bear arms 86

civil liberties, after September 11th attacks 95
Civil War 91
Clinton, Bill 37, **39,** *54,* 101, 119c
collective rights argument. *See* militia view
collectors 69
colonial America *10, 14m*
British anti-quartering laws 6
British origins of colonists 1
British quartering in 15–16, 18, 114c
British roots of Second and Third Amendment 8
gun ownership 9–12, **11**
gun ownership by Tories 13
limitations on gun ownership 11–13, **12**
militia 13, 15
Colorado state constitution 124
Columbine High School 76
Committee on Law Enforcement (American Bar Association) 116c
common law 1, 108g
computerized checking system 82, 119c
concealed carry laws 42, 42m, **73,** 108g
Concord, Massachusetts 18
Congress, U.S.
gun control activists in **83**
gun control laws 30, 32
Gun-Free Schools Act (1995) 38
interstate commerce **33**
Connecticut **11,** 28, 124
Connecticut Courant **24**
Constitutional Convention 21–22, 115c
Constitution of the United States ix, 122–123
arguments against gun control 85–87
Bill of Rights 25, 27–29, 123
debates over writing of 19
interstate commerce **33**
ratification 22–29, **25,** 26m, 115c
states' proposed amendments to **25**
Supreme Court challenges 46
United States v. Cruikshank **47**
Continental Congress, First 20, 114c
Continental Congress, Second 20

convicted felons
    Brady Bill 118*c*
    Federal Firearms Act 34
    Lewis v. United States 52, 53,
        117*c*
"cooling-off period" 89. *See also*
    waiting period
Copeland, Royal 34
cost, of medical care for firearms
    injuries 76
court cases 47–60
    Dred Scott v. Sandford 86
    Emerson v. United States 57–58,
        58
    Engblom v. Carey 61, **61,** 118*c*
    Kelley v. R.G. Industries 61
    Lewis v. United States **52,**
        52–53, 117*c*
    Miller v. Texas 50, 116*c*
    NAACP v. Accusport Inc. et al
        60, 120*c*
    naming of **45**
    Oregon State v. Kessler 61
    People v. Brown 60
    Presser v. State of Illinois 48,
        50, **50,** 116*c*
    Printz v. United States 53–54
    *Quilici v. Village of Morton
        Grove* 56–57
    Richardson v. Holland 61
    Salina v. Blaksley 60
    Schubert v. DeBard 61
    Second Amendment and 45–61
    Silveira v. Lockyer 58–59
    state court decisions 60–61
    State v. Buzzard 60
    Supreme Court decisions
        47–55
    Supreme Court's function
        45–47
    United States v. Bean 54–55
    United States v. Cruikshank
        47–48, 115*c*
    United States v. Lopez 53
    United States v. Miller 50–52,
        117*c*
    United States v. Tot 55–56, **56**
    *United States v. Verdugo-
        Urquidez* 86
    Warren v. District of Columbia 88
court decisions, application of **55**
Cox, Chris **104**
crime
    arguments against gun control
        87–89
    committed with firearms, sen-
        tencing for. *See* sentencing

gun control debate in 1920s 30
    Gun Free School Zones Act 38
    police response time to 88
    Prohibition 116*c*
    self-defense 77–78, 87–89
    tommy gun **31**
crimes committed with firearms
    70*t*
    Firearms Owners' Protection
        Act 118*c*
    Gun Control Act of 1968 117*c*
    sentencing for. *See* sentencing
crime victims
    criminals with firearms 69
    Gun Industry Responsibility
        Act 120*c*
    injuries suffered by 68*t*
criminals
    Brady Bill 118*c*
    deterrent 69
    gaining control of victim's
        weapon 77
    gun control laws 90
    gun use by. *See* illegal gun use
    purchases at gun shows 36
    restriction of gun ownership
        87
    sale of firearms to 116*c*
    sources of guns for 67*t*
Cromwell, Oliver 113*c*
crossbow 7
Cruikshank, William J. 47
culture, suicide rates and 89
Cummings, Homer **33**

D

Dallas, Texas 75
dealers. *See also* sales
    Firearms Owners' Protection
        Act 118*c*
    Gun Control Act of 1968 117*c*
    inventory rulings 99
    sales to terrorists 96, 99
    willingness to flout federal law
        90–91
deaths, firearms-related 76
Declaration of Independence *17,*
121
    Thomas Jefferson and 16
    quartering 18
    signing of 114*c*
    state constitutions **16**
Declaration of Rights (England) 6,
    6, 114*c*
Delaware **16,** 21, 124
Democratic Party 101
Dickinson, John 20

Disarmament Act (Brazil) 105
dishonorable discharge **98**
domestic violence 119*c*
Drain, James **87**
Dred Scott v. Sandford 86
drug dealers 118*c*
the Dutch 12–13, 113*c*

E

early America. *See* colonial Amer-
    ica
Eddie Eagle GunSafe Program 90,
    90
education, commerce and 53
Edward I (king of England) **7,**
    112*c*
Edward VI (king of England) 7,
    112*c*
effectiveness, of gun control laws
    90–91, **104**
Eighteenth Amendment **31,** 116*c*
elderly people 74
Emerson, Sacha 57–58
Emerson, Timothy Joe 57–58
Emerson v. United States 57–59, **58**
Engblom v. Carey 61, **61**
England
    forced quartering laws 111*c*
    Game Act 113*c*
    gun control laws 105
    gun sales to Native Americans
        12, 113*c*
    militia **2,** 111*c*
    murder rates 87
    need for professional army 4
    Norman conquest 111*c*
    origins of right not to quarter
        troops 4–6
    origins of right to bear arms
        1, 3–4, 7–8, **8**
    political philosophers **8**
    proposed international arms
        trade treaty 104
    Quartering Act of 1765 16, 18
    Quartering Act of 1774 18
    quartering in colonial America
        15–16, 18
    Saxon *fyrd* **2,** 111*c*
    standing army in American
        colonies 13, 15
    threat of colonial militia 15
English Settlement, 18th Century
    2*m*
Europe **23**
executive orders on assault
    weapons 37
"expectation of privacy" 61

F

family members, murder cases and 77
Federal Bureau of Investigation (FBI)
  background checks **98**
  burglary statistics 77
  counterterrorism system 97
  firearm use in robberies and assaults 69
  justifiable homicide statistics 68
  police fatalities and firearms 71
federal courts of appeal 55–60
Federal Firearms Act 33–36, 116*c*
Federal Firearms Transaction Record 97
federal government, U.S. 108*g*
  Articles of Confederation 20
  Constitutional Convention 21–22
  gun control laws 30–40
  interstate commerce **33**
  Miller v. Texas 116*c*
  Second Amendment as limitation of power of 48
  standing army 22
  state militias 22
  Supreme Court Cases **45**
  United States v. Cruikshank 115*c*
federal gun control laws 30–40
  after John F. Kennedy's assassination 35, 117*c*
  arguments for 79–82
  debate in 1920s 30
  interstate commerce **33**
federal gun laws, need for consistent 80
federalism **19, 22, 24**
The Federalist Papers **23,** 24
Federalists 21–24, 108*g*
felony. *See* convicted felons
Fifth Circuit Court of Appeals **55,** 58, 59
.50-caliber rifle 99–101, 108*g*
fingerprinting (of firearms). *See* ballistic fingerprinting
fingerprinting (of gun owners) 33, 81, **81**
firearms. *See* gun(s)
Firearms Acquisition Certificate (Canada) 105
firearms laws. *See* gun control laws
Firearms Owners' Protection Act 36, **36,** 118*c*

firearms statistics, difficulty in compiling 62
First Amendment 86
Fletcher, Andrew **8**
Florida 99, 124
forced quartering. *See* quartering
Ford, Gerald 78*t*
Foster, Sir Michael **87**
Franklin, Benjamin 22
funding, for gun control laws 54
future, of gun control issues 94–106
fyrd **3,** 108*g*, 111*c*

G

Game Act 113*c*
gangsters 30, *32,* 108*g*, 116*c*
Garfield, James 78*t*
George III (king of England) 15
Georgia 11, **57,** 119*c*, 124
German gun control laws 105
Geronimo *10*
Gerry, Elbridge **15,** 28, *28*
Great Britain. *See* England
Griffin, Thomas J. **65**
group rights, individual rights *vs.* xi–xiii
gun(s) *xiii. See also* handgun(s); rifle(s); shotgun(s)
  crimes committed with (1973–2001) 70*t*
  dealers. *See* dealers
  ease of killing with 78
  estimates of total number in United States 62, 64
  importance in colonial America 9
  increasing sophistication in 1700s 4
  murder weapon 70*t*–72*t*
  sales of. *See* sales
  smuggling 96
  sources, for criminals 67*t*
  types of **63**
gun clubs 33
Gun Control Act of 1968 35, 36, 117*c*, 118*c. See also* Omnibus Crime Control and Safe Streets Act
gun control (case against) 85–93
  advocacy groups 91–93
  assault weapons ban 101
  Charlton Heston **92**
  self-defense arguments 68–69
  United States v. Miller 52

gun control (case for) 75–84
  advocacy groups 83–84
  assault weapons ban 101
  Jim and Sarah Brady **39**
  congressional advocates **83**
  Emerson v. United States 58
  John Hinckley, Jr. 75–76
  self-defense arguments 67–68
  United States v. Miller 51–52
gun control laws 30–44
  arguments against. *See* gun control (case against)
  arguments favoring. *See* gun control (case for)
  background checks **98**
  Thomas Blanton on **32**
  Brady Bill 38, 40
  colonial America 11–13, 115*c*
  Homer Cummings on **33**
  effectiveness of 90–91, **104**
  England 112*c*, 113*c*
  executive orders on assault weapons 37
  Federal Firearms Act 33–34
  federal laws. *See* federal gun control laws
  Firearms Owners' Protection Act 36
  and gradual loss of rights 87
  Gun Control Act of 1968 35
  Gun-Free Schools Act (1995) 38
  Gun Free School Zones Act (1990) 37–38
  inefficacy of 90–91
  international 80, 96, 104–106
  interstate commerce 33, **33**
  Law Enforcement Officers Protection Act 35
  Massachusetts Bay Colony 114*c*
  Miller Act 32–33, 116*c*
  National Firearms Act 33
  Native Americans 10
  Omnibus Crime Control and Safe Streets Act 34–35
  permit process **81**
  politics of 101, 103
  public opinion and **73**
  "Roaring Twenties" 31, **31**
  Second Amendment 82–83
  state laws 40–44
  Statute of Northampton 112*c*
  terrorism 97, 99
  Undetectable Firearms Act 36
  Violent Crime Control and Law Enforcement Act 40

gun dealers. *See* dealers
Gun-Free Schools Act (1995) 38, 53, 119*c*
Gun Free School Zones Act (1990) 37–38, 53, 118*c*, 119*c*
Gun Industry Responsibility Act 120*c*
gun manufacturers
  Gun Industry Responsibility Act 120*c*
  lawsuits against **59, 73, 104,** 119*c*, 120*c*
  NAACP v. Accusport Inc. et al 60, 120*c*
  public opinion on lawsuits **73**
  Richardson v. Holland 61
  role and responsibility **103,** 103–104
gun ownership
  and break-ins 77
  burglary statistics 67
  colonial America 9–12
  firearms deaths 68
  mandatory. *See* mandatory weapons ownership
  suicide rates 79
Gun Owners of America 93
gun permit. *See* permit
gunpowder **63**
gun safety. *See* safety
gun sales. *See* sales
gun shows **36,** 108*g*
  background checks **98**
  criminals' purchases at 82
  Firearms Owners' Protection Act **36,** 118*c*
  Gun Industry Responsibility Act 120*c*
  terrorists' purchases at 99
gun skills 91
gun use, legal 64–69

H

Hamilton, Alexander 23, *24*
hand grenade 33
handgun(s)
  American Bar Association recommendations 116*c*
  Americans favoring registering of **73**
  barrel length **63**
  Canadian prohibition 87
  Emerson v. United States 58
  English prohibition 7, 105
  Firearms Owners' Protection Act 36

Gun Control Act of 1968 35
  interstate traffic in 79
  Kelley v. R.G. Industries 61
  mail-order sales **31,** 32–33, 116*c*
  Miller Act 32–33, 116*c*
  murder by (selected countries, 1998) 80*t*
  NAACP v. Accusport Inc. et al 60, 120*c*
  Omnibus Crime Control and Safe Streets Act 117*c*
  Quilici v. Village of Morton Grove 56, 57
  Russian prohibition 105
  self-defense against burglaries 77
  "smart gun" requirement 91
  suicide rates 79
  target shooting 65
  total number in United States 62
  United States v. Tot 55
  unlicensed 50
Handgun Control, Inc. **39,** 108*g*, 117*c*, 120*c*
handgun sales, multiple. *See* multiple firearms sales
Harris, Eric 76
Hartley, Thomas 28
Hawaii state constitution 124
Hemenway, David **79**
Henry, Patrick 22–23, *23*
Henry I (king of England) 5
Henry II (king of England) 7, 111*c*
Henry VII (king of England) 7
Henry VIII (king of England) 7, 112*c*
Heston, Charlton *92*, **92**
high school marksmanship students *37*
Hinckley, John, Jr. 38, **39, 75,** 75–76
Homeland Security Act **96**
homeowners, rights of ix–x, 69. *See also* Third Amendment
households, with handguns 79
House of Representatives, U.S. **83,** 97, 99
hunter *63*
hunting 9, **64,** 64–65
hunting license 65

I

Idaho state constitution 125
illegal gun use 69–74, 70*t*–72*t*

Illinois 56–57, 125
Independence Hall (Philadelphia, Pennsylvania) *22*
independence movement, American colonial 15
Independent Gazeteer 23
Indiana 61, 125
Indians, American. *See* Native Americans
individual rights view 109*g*
  Dred Scott v. Sandford 86
  group rights *vs.* xi–xiii
  NRA's Institute for Legislative Action 91
  Schubert v. DeBard 61
  Second Amendment xii–xiii, 85–86
  United States v. Verdugo-Urquidez 86
inefficacy, of gun control laws 90–91
injury, gun ownership and **77**
Injury Prevention (journal) 79
Institute for Legislative Action (ILA) 91
international arms trade treaty 104
international gun control laws 80, 96, 104–106
Internet, purchases over 82
interstate commerce **33,** 109*g*
  Firearms Owners' Protection Act 36, 118*c*
  Gun Control Act of 1968 35
  Gun-Free Schools Act (1995) 38, 119*c*
  Gun Free School Zones Act (1990) 37–38
  handguns 79
  Omnibus Crime Control and Safe Streets Act 35, 117*c*
  United States v. Lopez 53
inventory, by firearms dealers 99
Irish Republican Army (IRA) 96
Israeli gun control laws 105

J

Jackson, Andrew 78*t*
jail sentences. *See* sentencing
James II (king of England) 3, 6, 113*c*
Jamestown, Virginia 12, 112*c*
Jam Master Jay 78
Japan 89, 104, 105
Jay, John 23
Jefferson, Thomas 15, *16*
Johnson, Lyndon Baines 35

Journal of Clinical Psychiatry 89
Journal of the American Medical Association 76, 89
justifiable homicide 68
juvenile handgun possession 40, 43*m*

K

Kansas 60, 125
Kelley v. R.G. Industries 61
Kennedy, Edward F. **83**
Kennedy, John F. 34–35, 78*t*, **83**, 117*c*
Kennedy, Robert F. 34, *34,* 78*t*, **83,** 117*c*
Kennesaw, Georgia **57,** 69
Kentucky state constitution 125
King, Martin Luther, Jr. 34, *34,* 78, 117*c*
Kinkel, Kip 76–77
Klebold, Dylan 76
Kleck, Gary 69
knights 1, 111*c*
knives, as murder weapon 78

L

Lautenberg, Frank **97**
law. *See* court cases; gun control laws
Law Enforcement Officers Protection Act 35
law enforcement personnel, murder of 72*t*
Lawrence Research **73**
laws, gun control. *See* gun control laws
lawsuits, against gun manufacturers **59, 73,** 119*c*, 120*c*
Layton, Frank 50–52
"Learning and Defense Club" 48
Lee, Richard Henry **85,** *86*
legal gun use 64–69
Lennon, John 78
Lewis, George Calvin 52
Lewis v. United States **52,** 52–53, 117*c*
Lexington and Concord, Battle of 18, 114*c*
license fees 35, 38, 65, 117*c*
licensing 105
    Federal Firearms Act 34, 116*c*
    Firearms Owners' Protection Act 36, **36**
    Gun Control Act of 1968 35
    gun control advocates' stance 80–81

gun shows **36**
    laws in other countries 105–106
    state laws 41
licensing and registration laws, by state (2004) 41*m*
limitations, on right to bear arms. *See also* gun control laws
    colonial America 11–13, **12**
    England 7–8, **8**
    level of acceptance by gun control opponents 87
Lincoln, Abraham 78*t*
Littleton, Colorado 76
lobbying 83, 91, 93, 103
lobbyist 109*g*
London, England 4–5, 111*c*
longbows 112*c*
Lopez, Alfonso, Jr. 53
Louisiana 47, 125
lower court decisions 55–60
    Emerson v. United States 57–58, **58**
    Engblom v. Carey 61, **61**
    and militia view 82
    NAACP v. Accusport Inc. et al 60, 120*c*
    Quilici v. Village of Morton Grove 56–57
    Silveira v. Lockyer 58–59
    and Supreme Court decisions 47
    United States v. Tot 55–56, **56**
    Warren v. District of Columbia 88
Luxembourg gun control laws 105

M

Mach, Richard 54
machine gun. *See* tommy gun
Madison, James 23, **23,** 25, 27–28
magazine 40, 109*g*
Mailing of Firearms Act. *See* Miller Act
mail-order pistol sales **31,** 32–33, 116*c*
Maine state constitution 125
Malvo, Lee 76
mandatory weapons ownership
    colonial America 10–12, **11,** 112*c*
    England 6–7, 111*c*, 112*c*
    Kennesaw, Georgia **57**
manufacturing bans 116*c*
marksmanship *37,* 91

Mary I (queen of England) 7, 114*c*
Maryland
    Articles of Confederation 20
    Catholic gun ownership prohibition 12, 114*c*
    Kelley v. R.G. Industries 61
    quartering laws **16,** 21
Mary (queen of England, Scotland, and Ireland) 6
Mason, George 23
Massachusetts
    Bill of Rights 25
    quartering laws **16,** 21
    state constitution 125–126
    Third Amendment debate 28
Massachusetts Bay Colony **11,** 114*c*
McCarthy, Carolyn **83,** *98,* **98,** 103
McClure, James A. 36
McKinley, William 78*t*
medical costs, of firearms injuries 76
mentally disabled people
    background checks 82, **98**
    Brady Bill 38, 118*c*
    Gun Control Act of 1968 35, 117*c*
    John Hinckley, Jr. 38, **39, 75,** 75–76
    Long Island commuter train shooting **83**
    restriction of gun ownership to 87
    state laws 42, 44
    suicide rates 89
Metaksa, Tanya **36**
metal detectors 36, 94, 118*c*
Mexico 54–55, 104
Michigan 60, 126
Middle Ages 1
militia 109*g*
    African Americans 12
    Articles of Confederation 20–21, 115*c*
    Sir William Blackstone on **8**
    colonial America 11, 13, 15
    Constitution 22, **25**
    England 1–4, 6, 113*c*
    Lexington and Concord, Battle of 114*c*
    New York State **13**
    Presser v. State of Illinois 116*c*
    quartering 16
    ratification debate 22–24
    Saxon *fyrd* **2, 3,** 111*c*
    Uniform Militia Act 115*c*
    Virginia laws **16,** 21

Militia Act (England) 2, 3, 113*c*
Militia Ordinance 113*c*
militia view 48, *49*, 109*g*
   Presser v. State of Illinois 48, 50
   Quilici v. Village of Morton Grove 57
   Salina v. Blaksley 60
   Second Amendment xii, 30, 48, 50, 82, 85
   Silveira v. Lockyer 59
   state court decisions 60
   State v. Buzzard 60
   United States v. Miller 51, 52
   United States v. Tot 56
Miller, Franklin P. 50
Miller, Jack 50–52
Miller, John 32–33
Miller Act 32–33, 116*c*
Miller v. Texas 50, 116*c*
Million Mom March **80,** 84, 119*c*
minorities, denial of gun ownership to 87
missiles 33
Missouri 61, 126
Montana 54, 126
Morton Grove, Illinois 56, 57
Muhammad, John 76
multiple firearms sales 38, 97, 99
murder
   committed with firearms (2003 survey) 69, 71
   gun control debate in 1920s 30
   by handguns 80*t*
   involving family or friends 77
   law enforcement personnel (1973-2000) 72*t*
   rates of 80, 89
   weapons used for 70*t*, 71*t*
musket 10–11
muster 109*g*

N

NAACP v. Accusport Inc. et al 60, 120*c*
National Archives (Washington, D.C.) ix
National Association for the Advancement of Colored People (NAACP) 60
National Center for Health Statistics 73–74
National Center for Injury Prevention and Control (NCIPC) 90
National Council to Control Handguns 117*c*

National Firearms Act 33, 50, 51, 116*c*, 117*c*
National Guard 61, *95*, 109*g*, 115*c*
National Guard recruiting poster *xi*
National Instant Check System 119*c. See also* computerized checking system
National Opinion Research Center **73**
National Rifle Association (NRA) 109*g*
   American households with firearms 64
   Eddie Eagle GunSafe Program 90, **90**
   Charlton Heston and **92**
   lobbying by 103
   number of firearms in United States 62
   opposition to Federal Firearms Act 33
   political influence 103
   statistics on hunters 64
   target shooting statistics 65
   wildlife conservation 65
National Shooting Sports Foundation 93, 104
National Vital Statistics Report 77
Native Americans 9–12, **12,** 87, 112*c*–115*c*
Navy, U.S. (recruiting poster) *27*
Nebraska state constitution 126
Nelson, Levi 47
Nevada state constitution 126
Newark, New Jersey 55
New Hampshire **16, 25,** 126
New Mexico state constitution 126
New York, colony of **11,** 12–13, 113*c*
New York City 79, **81,** 120*c*
New York City Police Department 79, **81**
New York Journal 22
New York State
   Bill of Rights 25, **25**
   Engblom v. Carey 61
   militia 13, 21
   NAACP v. Accusport Inc. et al 60
New York Times 89
1920s 30, **31**
Ninth Circuit Court of Appeals **55,** 59
nobility, English 1, 2
Normans 1, 2, 111*c*
Northampton, Statute of (England) 7, 112*c*

North Carolina 25, **25,** 127
North Dakota state constitution 127
Northern Ireland 96

O

Ohio state constitution 127
Oklahoma state constitution 127
Olympic Games 65, **65**
Omnibus Crime Control and Safe Streets Act 34–35, 52–53, 117*c*
opinion, Supreme Court 46–47
Oregon 61, 127
Oregon State v. Kessler 61
Our Lady of Peace Act **98**

P

Parliament 2, **5,** 5–6, 112*c*, 113*c*
parts, of guns **33**
Patriots 5
Pennsylvania
   amendments to U.S. Constitution **25**
   quartering laws **16**
   right to bear arms 21
   Second Amendment debate 28
   state constitution arms provisions 127
   Third Amendment debate 28
Pentagon terrorist attacks. *See* September 11, 2001, terrorist attacks
"people," use of term in Second Amendment 85–86
People v. Brown 60
permit
   Americans favoring requirement **73**
   Federal Firearms Act 34
   New York City **81**
   revocation 88
   state laws 41–42
   Switzerland 106
personal responsibility, gun safety and 90
Philadelphia, Pennsylvania 21, 114*c*, 115*c*
pistol(s). *See* handgun(s)
pistol competitions 91
plastic guns 36, 118*c*
Plymouth colony **11,** 112*c*
police
   deaths by own weapon 77
   deterrent to crime 88
   England 6

murder of 71, 72*t*
understaffing 88
political philosophers, English **8**
politics, gun control and 101, 103
post-Revolutionary America 20–29
pre-Revolutionary America 14*m*
presidents (U.S.),
    assassinations/attempted assassi-
    nations 78*t*
the press, ratification debate and
    22–24
Presser, Herman 48
Presser v. State of Illinois 48, 50,
    50, 57, 116*c*
Printz, Jay 54
Printz v. United States 53–54
prison guards 118*c*
private sales of weapons 36. *See
    also* gun shows
privileges, rights *vs.* 86–87
product liability law 103
Prohibition **31,** 116*c*
Project Exile 91
protection, gun ownership for. *See*
    self-defense
Protection of Lawful Commerce in
    Arms Act 104
public figures, assassinations and
    78–79
public opinion **73,** 103
purchases, limitation of 99
Purdy, Patrick 37

Q
al-Qaeda 96
quartering 109*g*. *See also* Third
    Amendment
    amendments to Constitution
        25
    Anti-Quartering Act (England)
        113*c*
    British, in colonial America
        15–16, 18, 114*c*
    England 4–6, 111*c*, 113*c*
    in peace and wartime 28
    state laws **16,** 21
Quartering Act of 1765 16, 18
Quartering Act of 1774 18
Quilici, Victor D. 56
Quilici v. Village of Morton Grove
    56–57
Quincy, Josiah 13

R
racism 47
ratification 22–29, **25,** 26*m*, 109*g*

Reagan, Ronald *75,* 78*t*
    assassination attempt 75–76
    on assault rifle ban **37**
    James Brady and **39**
    Brady Bill 38
    on gun control laws **36**
record-keeping 36, 118*c*
recovery, from suicide attempts
    79
recruiting poster, World War II *27*
redcoats *5,* 15, 16, 109*g*, 114*c*
registration 109*g*
    Americans favoring require-
        ment **73**
    Canada 87
    under Edward VI 112*c*
    English gun owners 7
    Federal Firearms Act 33–34
    laws in other countries
        105–106
    national system 81, 82
    state laws 41
regulation. *See* gun control laws
religion 28
renewal, of gun licenses 81
Republican Party **39,** 101
requirement to bear arms **11**
resale, of guns **73,** 82. *See also*
    gun shows
response time, of police 88
restraining order 58
Revolutionary War **19,** 20, 114*c*.
    See also American Revolution
revolver **63,** 117*c*. *See also* hand-
    gun
Rhode Island 25, 127
Richard II (king of England) 7,
    112*c*
Richardson v. Holland 61
Richmond, Virginia 91
rifle(s) **63**
    Americans favoring registra-
        tion **73**
    Canada 87
    .50-caliber 99–101, 108*g*
    Firearms Owners' Protection
        Act 36, 118*c*
    Great Britain 105
    Gun Control Act of 1968 35
    high-powered 99–101
    Law Enforcement Officers Pro-
        tection Act 35
    *Quilici v. Village of Morton
        Grove* 57
    target shooting 65
    Violent Crime and Law
        Enforcement Act 40

"Roaring Twenties" **31**
robbery 69
Rocky's Pawn Shop (Dallas, Texas)
    75
Roosevelt, Franklin Delano 33, *79*
Roosevelt, Theodore **64,** 78*t*
Roper Center for Public Opinion
    Research **73**
royal charter 4–5
royal power 3–4
Run DMC 78
Russia 105

S
safety devices *40*
safety instruction 81, 90, **90**
sales (of firearms). *See also* dealers
    criminals 116*c*
    mail-order **31,** 32–33, 116*c*
    multiple 38, 97, 99
    Native Americans **12,** 112*c*,
        113*c*
    private sales 36. *See also* gun
        shows
    resale **73**
    terrorists 96, 99
Salina v. Blaksley 60
San Antonio, Texas 53
saturday night specials 35, 38, 61,
    109*g*, 117*c*
sawed-off shotguns 33, 50–52,
    109*g*, 116*c*, 117*c*
Saxon *Fyrd* **3,** 111*c*
Saxons 1, **2**
school aid, federal 38, 53
schools, guns in 38
school shootings 37, 76–77
school zone 37, 38, 118*c*
Schubert v. DeBard 61
screening machines. *See* metal
    detectors
Second Amendment ix, xi–xiii,
    30–44, 82–83, 123
    arguments against gun control
        85–87
    court cases 45–61. *See also*
        lower court decisions;
        Supreme Court decisions
    current issues 94–106
    as guarantee of limits of gov-
        ernment power 85
    gun control debate in 1920s
        30
    historical limitations of 82
    Homeland Security Act and
        96

passage of 25, 27–28
post–September 11th 95
ratification debate 29
state court decisions 60–61
state law 50
Second Amendment Foundation
92–93
Second Circuit Court of Appeals
61
security checks, airport 94. *See
also* metal detectors
self-defense
argument against gun control
87–89
burglar's quote on guns and **76**
colonial America 9
crime 77–78
crime victims 68*t*
current issues 65–69
Sir Michael Foster on right of
87
Oregon State v. Kessler 61
public opinion **73**
semiautomatic 109*g*
semiautomatic weapons. *See*
assault weapons
sentencing
Firearms Owners' Protection
Act 36
Gun Control Act of 1968 35
gun control opponents' view
88
Project Exile 91
public opinion **73**
September 11, 2001, terrorist
attacks 94, 94–95
serial numbers 34, 41
Seventh Circuit U.S. Court of
Appeals 56
Seven Years' War (French and
Indian War) 15
"shall issue" states 42
Sherman, Roger 28
shooting practice. *See* target shooting
shootings, accidental. *See* accidents
shotgun(s) **63,** 109*g*
Canada 87
Firearms Owners' Protection
Act 36, 118*c*
Great Britain 105
Gun Control Act of 1968 35
*Quilici v. Village of Morton
Grove* 57
sawed-off 33, 50–52, 109*g*,
116*c*, 117*c*

shows. *See* gun shows
Siebel, Brian **103**
silencers 33
Silveira v. Lockyer 58–59
Silveira, Sean 59
slaves/slavery 12, 115*c*
smart gun 91, **100,** 109*g*
Smith, Edie **80**
Smith and Wesson 119*c*
smuggling 96
soldier *31. See also* quartering
South America 104
South Carolina 12, 28, 127
South Dakota state constitution
128
southern United States, handgun
purchases in 79
sovereign 2
Sporting Arms and Ammunition
Manufacturers 33
Springfield, Oregon 76–77
stalking 118*c*
standing army 1, 3–4, *27,* 110*g*
in American colonies 13, 15
Constitutional provisions 22,
25
Declaration of Rights provision 114*c*
in England 2, 4, 113*c*
James II and 113*c*
state constitutions
bills of rights in 24
gun laws 40–44
quartering laws **16**
right to bear arms **17,** 66,
66*m,* 123–128
state conventions, for ratification
of Constitution 24–25, **25**
state court decisions 60–61
Kelley v. R.G. Industries 61
Oregon State v. Kessler 61
People v. Brown 60
Richardson v. Holland 61
Salina v. Blaksley 60
Schubert v. DeBard 61
State v. Buzzard 60
State Department, U.S. 100
state governments xii, 20–21, 85
state gun laws 30, 40–44, 117*c*
after John F. Kennedy's assassination 117*c*
debate in 1920s 30
gun proliferation and 79, 80
New York *vs.* southern U.S. 79
*Quilici v. Village of Morton
Grove* 57
Second Amendment and 48

state militia. *See* militia
states' righters/states' rights 28,
82, 110*g*
Articles of Confederation 20,
21
Constitutional Convention
21–23
federal power *vs.* **19**
Miller v. Texas 116*c*
Presser v. State of Illinois 116*c*
United States v. Cruikshank
115*c*
State v. Buzzard 60
Statute of Winchester **7,** 112*c*
Stillman, Samuel 15
Stockton, California, school shooting 37
stolen weapons 67–68
storage, of guns 43
submachine gun. *See* tommy gun
suicide
arguments against gun control
89–90
arguments for gun control 79
gun prevalence and 73–74, **79**
Sumter, Thomas 28
Supreme Court *46*
debate over meaning of "the
right to bear arms" 47
function of 45–47
Gun Free School Zones Act
(1990) 38, 118*c*
militia view 82
Supreme Court decisions 47–55
Dred Scott v. Sandford 86
Emerson v. United States 58
Lewis v. United States **52,**
52–53, 117*c*
Miller v. Texas 50, 116*c*
Presser v. State of Illinois 48,
50, **50,** 116*c*
Printz v. United States 53–54
*Quilici v. Village of Morton
Grove* 56
Second Amendment decisions
47–55
United States v. Bean 54–55
United States v. Cruikshank
47–48, 115*c*
United States v. Lopez 53
United States v. Miller 50–52,
117*c*
*United States v. Verdugo-
Urquidez* 86
suspicion, of crime 97
Swiss Arms Act 106
Switzerland 88–89, 106

T

target shooting *64,* 65, **65**
taxation
    Articles of Confederation 21
    of firearms and ammunition
        65
    Medieval England 1
    National Firearms Act 33,
        116*c*
Tennessee state constitution 128
terrorists/terrorism 95–97, **96, 97,**
    99–100
Texas 50, 57–58, 128
theft, of guns 67
Third Amendment ix–x, 123
    after September 11th 95
    Engblom v. Carey 61, **61,** 118*c*
    ratification debate 28–29
    royal charters 4
Third Circuit Court of Appeals 56
Thompson, John T. **31**
Thurston High School 76–77
Tillman, Alexander 47
tommy gun(s) **31,** 33, 110*g,* 116*c*
Tories 13, 110*g*
Tot, Frank 55–56
trigger lock *40,* 43
Trinidad and Tobago 99
Truman, Harry S. 78*t*
tyranny 4, 13, 15, 24

U

unconstitutionality, of gun control
    laws 30, 46
understaffing, of police forces 88
Undetectable Firearms Act 36,
    118*c*
Uniform Crime Reports of the FBI
    68
Uniform Militia Act 115*c*
United Nations 104
United States v. Bean 54–55

United States v. Cruikshank **47,**
    47–48, 115*c*
United States v. Lopez 53
United States v. Miller 50–52, 56,
    117*c*
United States v. Tot 55–56, **56**
United States v. Verdugo-Urquidez
    86
University of California 68, 79,
    90–91
U.S. Department of Justice 69, 77,
    88
Utah state constitution 128

V

Vermont state constitution 128
vest, bulletproof 35
victims of crime. *See* crime victims
Violence Policy Center (VPC) 84
Violent Crime Control and Law
    Enforcement Act 37, 40, 119*c*
Virginia
    African-American gun owner-
        ship 12, 113*c,* 114*c*
    amendments to U.S. Constitu-
        tion **25**
    Bill of Rights 25
    colonial gun requirements 11
    early quartering laws **16**
    militia provision **16,** 21
    Native American gun owner-
        ship 114*c*
    state constitution 128
Volstead Act 116*c. See also* Eigh-
    teenth Amendment
voluntary quartering 5

W

waiting period 110*g*
    Americans favoring require-
        ment **73**
    background checks 82

Brady Bill 38, 82, 118*c,* 119*c*
suicide rates 89
suspected terrorists 99
Wallace, George 78*t*
War for Independence. *See* Ameri-
    can Revolution
Warren v. District of Columbia 88
Washington, D.C. **39,** 84, 119*c*
Washington, D.C., sniper killings
    76
Washington state gun laws 128
weapons, used for murder (2002)
    70*t*
Webster, Noah 24
West, Richard **1**
West Virginia state constitution
    128
wheelock 7, 110*g*
Wiebe, Douglas J. **77**
William of Orange (William III,
    king of England) 6, 114*c*
Wisconsin state constitution 128
women, colonial gun laws and 12
World Trade Center attacks. *See*
    September 11, 2001, terrorist
    attacks
World War II recruiting poster *27*
Wyoming state constitution 128

Y

young people
    firearms accidents (2000) 77
    firearms deaths in U.S. 76
    gun safety for **90**
    suicides involving firearms
        73–74